using Counselling Skills
on the Telephone

WITHDRAWN

Pete Sanders

PCCS BOOKS
Manchester

D1613017

First Published in 1993
PCCS BOOKS
3 Chelford Rd
Manchester
M16 0BJ

An Incomplete Guide to Using Counselling Skills on the Telephone

ISBN   1 898059 00 4

Cover Design by Peter Kneebone
Printed by Printoff Graphic Arts Ltd. Alexander House,
Lomeshaye Road. Nelson, Lancashire.

Contents

Contents

Contents

Introduction

The idea for this book grew out of the 1990 NAYPCAS (now Youth Access) Conference at St Martin's College, Lancaster. I was the tutor serving the Counselling Skills Phase 1 workshop that year and things were going well, I was in bouyant mood. Rather than use my free afternoon to take a rest I decided to offer a 'swopshop' session - sharing ideas, problems, solutions, issues, training interventions etc - on the topic of using counselling skills on the telephone.

It had struck me for some time that although the agencies affiliated to NAYPCAS were predominantly telephone agencies, there was no particular attention paid to telephone work at the conference. Since my own first counselling work was for a telephone agency and I had further experience of both working for and running training for telephone agencies, I thought I would put matters to rights and run a session off the cuff. It's good to be able to report that after 17 years as a counsellor trainer, the feeling of breath taking adventure when flying by the seat of your pants never leaves you.

Two NAYPCAS conferences later at which I ran 'proper' workshops on using counselling skills on the telephone, I have succumbed to participants' nudges in the "You-should-write-a-book" direction. This book, then, is all I know about using counselling skills on the telephone. I have learned it all by listening to other people and to myself. You can check, challenge, add and delete by the same method.

Using the metaphor of a journey when writing about counselling is not a new idea. I use it in several places throughout this book. The thing about journeys is that we all start from different places and even if we cover the same territory as other people, we each see the scenery through our own eyes, are excited by different things and take home different memories. This Incomplete Guide is your companion on this journey. It will point out some well-known landmarks and suggest some parts of town that are best avoided. However, because we all tackle journeys differently, some readers may well be attracted to what I consider to be the more dangerous areas.

If you are a newcomer to counselling and/or telephone work don't be put off by anything you read. Check it out yourself and add your experience to the guide.

Pete Sanders
Manchester

1 Useful Questions

The Most Useful Question

As counsellors we are used to doing our business face-to-face. Unless we are born blind we learn nearly all of our relationship skills through our primary sense of vision and many counselling texts refer to the special role of sight in 'active listening'. In fact counsellors pride themselves on the quality of this person-to-person contact.

When thinking about counselling on the telephone most people, including many experienced counsellors, go glassy eyed and muse about differences, difficulties and complications. We get distracted when the familiar ingredients in our tried and trusted counselling recipes are taken away. It reminds me of asking for a vegetarian meal in a restaurant 10 years ago and getting meat and two veg without the meat. Do we offer the same to our telephone clients?

During a workshop on telephone skills I wondered why our counselling marbles fly straight out of the window when we lose visual contact with our clients, that is, every time we pick up the phone. So we brainstormed the most common issues that arise around telephone work. As we 'stormed' and scribbled on our flipchart one question kept cropping up again and again. As each pitfall and issue concerning telephone work was highlighted, the same question returned in our minds and on our flipcharts. We soon realised that this was The Most Useful Question we could ask ourselves.

It was so simple and obvious. It led our thinking somewhere positive in every case. It untangled knots all over the place. Whether the problem was what to do with people who wanted us to talk to them while they masturbated, what to do when clients go silent, what to do with 'hoaxers', third party calls or what the limits of confidentiality are in the 'real world', the same question helped us get our counselling marbles back in place, and our thinking back on track.

The Most Useful Question is

What would I do in this situation if it were face-to-face?

We played for ages with this question. It helped us look at issues from a perspective which wasn't clouded by telephone terror, it gave an extra dimension to our discussion and it had its funny side when applied to popular 'telephone teasers'. Try it yourself for a bit before moving on to some more useful questions. Try it in training sessions, when discussing professional or ethical issues in telephone work and try asking yourself this question when you get in a tight spot on the phone with a client.

More Useful Questions (but not quite as useful as The Most Useful Question)

What are the advantages of telephone counselling?

Maybe you haven't thought about the advantages of telephone counselling before. Take a moment to think about the question.

> **In Training** : split the group into threes or fours and ask them to brainstorm answers to the question. Feedback and collate answers. Discuss.

Most people immediately make the assumption that the telephone is somehow second best or that real counselling can only be done face-to-face.

Many agencies have specific policies which implicitly accept, support and promote this assumption. They instruct volunteers to talk to callers only as long as it takes to persuade (in a non-directive way of course) the caller to visit the agency's premises for face-to-face counselling.

So what *are* the advantages then? Well it very much depends upon your personal/agency circumstances - some benefit clients, whilst others benefit counsellors/agencies. Here are a few to get you going:

• Convenient for client.

• Client is not seen, ie anonymous.

• Needs less accommodation.

• Doesn't need an appointments system.

• Location and environment are less important.

• Better personal safety for counsellors.

• Counsellor anonymity if required.

• Counsellor can make notes as a memory aid.

Why do people use telephone counselling services rather than see a counsellor face-to-face?

> **In Training** : split the group into threes and fours then ask them to brainstorm answers. Feedback and collate answers then discuss.
>
> This can be a good exercise in empathy with clients.

1. There are several external reasons why people may choose the telephone.

*By 'external' I mean some obstacle which lies outside the control of the individual. Some people do not have the flexibility and freedom in their lives to visit a counsellor.

> Single parents with young children, disabled people, people living in remote areas, people caring for disabled or infirm relatives, those who find transport difficult, or those whose personal freedom is restricted by another person as with abused women or children; the list is endless.

2. There are some internal or psychological reasons why people may choose the telephone.

*Counsellors are very concerned to offer a relationship that is as near to a partnership of equals as can be achieved. Most agencies offering counselling services, telephone or otherwise, try to make this very clear in their publicity. Yet we all know that out there in the 'real world' many people just do not know what we are offering.

 • A telephone is a low-risk way of testing the counsellor (and counselling) out.

*For some people, going to a counsellor would carry too much social stigma for them to bear or they might feel that it would be too great a sign of weakness.

 • The telephone gives some power back to such people. They may feel more in control if they can remain anonymous or put the receiver down and withdraw from the session without embarrassment or explanation.

*Others may not want to be 'seen'. Maybe they suffer from acute social embarrassment or they cannot face the thought of their 'problem' being made visible (even to themselves) by declaring it in the presence of another person.

 • The telephone affords a more comfortable halfway house for these people.

Some people are just too plain frightened to *go* to a doctor, counsellor or agency for help. They need the security that being able to use the telephone (possibly in the safety of their own home) gives them.

 • The telephone is a safe way of making contact contact with strangers or specialist helpers without actually having to *meet* them.

Are there any disadvantages to telephone counselling?

At last! Your opportunity to say how important all of those visual cues are. Face-to-face sighted counselling *is different* from telephone counselling, and it does have its disadvantages. I'll leave you to fill in the details on the obvious first disadvantage:

• The counsellor and client cannot make visual contact.

• The caller can terminate the session at any time and may do this impulsively to avoid tackling important issues.

• There are potentially more distractions and interruptions when working on the phone, for both the client and the counsellor.

• It's not possible to ensure the client's privacy on the 'phone.

How does telephone counselling differ from face-to-face counselling ?

Again, it's a rather obvious point to make, but you can't see who you're talking to on the phone. This gives rise to a number of special considerations regarding telephone work. Also, the telephone gives a different set of 'relationship tools' to those making the call than we are accustomed to in face-to-face interactions. This gives rise to another set of special considerations.

These special considerations can be looked at in two sets.

1. Differences due to the fact that you can't see who you're talking to:

* Every time the phone rings, the counsellor never knows whether they have spoken to the caller before or not. It might be a regular client or a first interview. This is in contrast to all but the most drop-in of face-to-face services.

* Confidentiality is an issue in all counselling settings, and in telephone counselling at the moment (technological advances may soon change this) both the client and counsellor have complete

control over their identities and their location. The caller can remain anonymous throughout the relationship if they so choose.

* Counsellors can also remain anonymous. Indeed this is often a requirement in many agencies. A counsellor may find this an awkward boundary which may get in the way of them forming a good relationship with their client. Other counsellors may feel more secure and relaxed in this anonymity.

•The two points above have an effect on both client and counsellor judgements, since we form some very durable impressions on first *sight*.
Economic status, social class, gender, racial origin etc are all things we are likely to make guesses about as a result of how people look.

•When we can't see the person we are talking to we use a different set of cues - accent, dialect, tone of voice, pitch of voice etc. Some of these judgements we make on first *hearing* may be completely different from those we make at first *sight*.

> **In Training** : A useful exercise is to play a tape of different people saying a fixed sentence then getting trainees to give each voice a 'life story' with lots of demographic detail - name age, gender, job (or not), ethnic origin, sexual orientation etc.

* Telephone counselling can require more concentration than face-to-face counselling because the counsellor is working 'blind' and has to work with a more limited range of cues. This extra effort can make the whole business much more exhausting than face-to-face work. (See Chapters 6 & 7)

2. Differences due to a new set of 'relationship tools':

When I talk about 'relationship tools', I mean those factors that we use in the management of relationships which rely on us being in the same room as the other person for example, or the rules of politeness or courtesy which have grown up with telephone use. Also we have a history in our culture of using the 'phone as a 'quick-fix' solution, or message channel when face-to-face can't be achieved. Sometimes it is seen as a second best option. This affects some of the ways we use counselling on the 'phone and some of the ways clients behave.

* In telephone counselling the counsellor has less control over some aspects of the relationship than in face-to-face counselling. On the 'phone, clients can virtually start and stop the session when they please.

* In most face-to-face counselling settings, the sessions are of a roughly pre-determined length, whereas in most telephone counselling settings the call is of variable length and may in some agencies be unlimited. (Some agencies have a policy that ensures that only the client can terminate contact. This can lead to some very long calls (See Chapters 6 & 7)

*The client may expect the telephone service offered by an agency or individual as a preliminary to the 'real' face-to-face counselling. This means that they may never really get started, preferring to leave the 'real stuff' for the face-to-face session.

*Many telephone counselling relationships can be one call only. The caller is likely to call once and never again. Face-to-face relationships more often last for a few sessions spread over some weeks, and occasionally many sessions over a period of months. Telephone work is much shorter term, with a relationship lasting weeks or months being the exception rather than the rule.

Possibly the Most Important Question

Is it *possible* to do counselling on the telephone?

You may be wondering why I have left this Most Important Question until last. You will also realise that it would be silly of me to write a Guide to doing something that I thought was impossible! There are, however, several books which never seem to consider the possibility that counselling can take place in anything other than face-to-face contexts and others which actually build in face-to-face contact as a requirement in their definition of counselling.

I have left this question until last because the answer is tied up with the next chapter in which I look at some definitions of counselling. If we can define counselling and identify its key ingredients, then as long as being face-to-face with the client isn't one of them, we must be able to do it on the phone.

> **In Training** : Split group into twos and threes and ask the question: Is it an essential condition of counselling that the counsellor and client have
> to   a) be able to see the client or
>   b) be in the same room as the client?
>
> Feed back, collate answers and discuss.

I sometimes have to remind myself that a couple of the best counsellors I know are blind or visually challenged. How do *they* do it if sighted, face-to-face contact is a requirement?

As I've mentioned above, being unsighted is not the only difference between telephone and face-to-face counselling, so maybe some definitions would have other objections to the telephone. If they do, then I haven't come across them yet. I find Stephen Murgatroyd's book **Counselling and Helping** very good for clarifying some issues. He says that it's the idea of what the *nature of the helping is* that should guide our thinking on definitions. He points out that we should not think that 'counselling is what counsellors do', rather counselling is a certain form of helping with certain aims and possible outcomes. These aims can be held, and these outcomes achieved, by a wide range of people. I would add to that 'in a wide range of situations, *including over the telephone*'.

One thing which does separate counselling from other types of helping is the ethical positions and professional standards within, and towards, which counsellors choose to work. Again, I have neither read nor experienced anything yet which leads me to believe that the telephone might compromise my work ethically or professionally. That doesn't mean to say that the telephone hasn't provided me with many ethical challenges , but none that supervision has failed to cope with to date.

What about all the other questions?

One of the things I find about questions is that they breed like flies. Once I start, I can't stop. Another problem with questions is that I nearly always seem to get a flood of ideas at rather inconvenient moments, but I have found it helpful to try to record my questions as soon as possible, otherwise I forget them.

*If you have any more questions:

  • Write them down.

  • Ask them at the next opportunity whether it be a
  training session, supervision session, or with fellow
  counsellors when you next meet (maybe on duty
  between calls).

*All the other questions I could think of asking are asked throughout the rest of the Guide. I do my best to share the answers I've found most useful. Most have been thought up by other people in the course of their struggle to get better at telephone counselling.

2 Necessary Definitions

Some Definitions

1. Counselling

At some point its always useful to define the terms you're using and I have found it increasingly important over the years to define *counselling*. Counselling has become one of the most over used, badly defined and misunderstood terms in the past 15 years.

It has been used to describe any kind of tutorial or advice situation in education, through various psychotherapies and helping relationships to disciplinary hearings. In the forces and in some medical settings you are said to have been 'counselled' when you have been cautioned or ticked off!

In Training: A popular way to start a counselling skills training programme is to ask trainees to define counselling. Collate the definitions or key words/concepts on a flip chart. Then discuss.

Defining the activity is important because we need to put boundaries around activities sometimes and counselling is one of those activities. We need to know its rough position in the 'helping firmament' before we can put those boundaries in place. We need to know whether we are giving information, counselling, advising, or befriending at any given time.

So how can we separate counselling from other forms of helping relationship? What are the distinguishing features of counselling? Is there only one type of counselling and do you have to do a special sort of counselling on the telephone?

The British Association for Counselling say in their **Code of Ethics and Practice for Counsellors** :

> "The term 'counselling' includes work with individuals, pairs or groups of people, often, but not always, referred to as 'clients'.
>
> Counselling may be concerned with developmental issues, addressing and resolving specific problems, making decisions, coping with crisis, developing personal insight and knowledge, working through feelings of inner conflict or improving relationships with others. The counsellor's role is to facilitate the client's work in ways which respect the client's values, personal resources and capacity for self-determination.
>
> Only when both the user and recipient explicitly agree to enter into a counselling relationship does it become 'counselling' rather than the use of 'counselling skills'."

Francesca Inskipp, in her **Counselling : The Trainer's Handbook**, defines counselling as :

" a) providing help and support and an understanding listener for someone who is concerned or perplexed;

  b) creating a climate so that the 'client' feels accepted, non-defensive and able to talk freely about himself and his feelings (begins to build a trusting relationship);

  c) helping the client to gain clearer insight into himself

and his situation so that he is better able to help himself and draw on his resources." (p 21)

I have mentioned in Chapter 1 that Stephen Murgatroyd suggests that it may be important to focus on the nature of the helping process rather than the qualifications or professional standing of the helper. In the same way that healing is the process of being made well and not just the thing that happens to you when you go to a healer, then counselling is the process whereby:

* clients are given an opportunity to explore and discover ways of living more resourcefully;

* clients are assisted in the exploration of their world;

* helped to explore their understanding of things that are troubling them;

* enabled to achieve a greater sense of self-determination.

This process could conceivably happen in a number of settings. There are two elements in a definition of counselling: i)*the process* and ii)*the context* in which the process takes place. Both are required before the activity can be properly named. The features which make a counselling context particular are:

• At least two people are required. One must identify themselves as in need of help (the client) the other must identify themselves as the person providing help (the counsellor).

• The participants must be in psychological contact. (Some helping activities can be done by post for example, but not counselling)

• Both counsellor and client must identify the process as *counselling* rather than some other helping relationship.

• Counselling is freely entered into by the person seeking help.
• The counsellor acknowledges the central role of, and actively uses, relationship variables in the counselling process.

• The counsellor will share with the client the common key purpose of the activity. (To help the client through counselling.)

Other types of helping relationship commonly compared with counselling are Advice, Guidance, Befriending and Mentoring/Tutoring.

Advising helps the client develop problem solving, increase choices, options and possible actions by providing information appropriate to the client's needs.

Guiding gives the client access to the increased options and information (above in advising) and enables the client to make informed choices by exploring their concerns and developing decision making skills.

In **Befriending**: we provide support to distressed people for as long as it may be required. A befriending relationship has an 'everyday' quality to it and will help the person feel more supported and less isolated.

The terms **Mentoring and Tutoring** refer to activities within an educational setting which are concerned with:
i) providing a safe and supportive learning environment,
ii) enabling a learner, student or trainee to construct and manage their own learning environment to meet their own individual learning needs, or
iii) advising or guiding the student within that student managed learning environment.

For further information on the differentiation between Counselling, Counselling Skills, Advice, and Guidance, copies of the Differentiation Project Report and Summary Report of the Advice, Guidance and Counselling Lead Body are available from the address given in the Appendix

2. Using Counselling Skills

Quite apart from a definition of the context, aims and objectives of counselling as well as the process of counselling, we encounter another notion which recurs in many texts. This is that there should be a distinction between counselling and the use of counselling skills. The difference being that counselling is what counsellors do and counselling skills can be used by anyone in a helping relationship or alongside an already well developed set of professional skills such as nursing, teaching, youth work, social work etc.

So what makes a counsellor different from any other type of helper, professional or voluntary? Much has been written about this in the last twenty years and this is where the British Association for Counselling comes in again. Their **Code of Ethics and Practice for Counsellors** is an attempt to bring together many diverse schools and approaches to counselling under one set of professional aims and responsibilities. The BAC also publish a **Code of Ethics and Practice for Counselling Skills** which applies to BAC members who use counselling skills to support their roles.

It could be said then, that a counsellor is someone who practices counselling skills whilst abiding by the BAC Code of Ethics and Practice or an equivalent professional code. My own definition is:

> Counselling Skills are interpersonal communication skills derived from the study of therapeutic change in human beings, used in a manner consistent with the goals and values of the established ethics of the profession of the practitioner in question. In addition, the user of counselling skills will find that their own professional skills are enhanced by the process.

This would then allow teachers, clergy, youth workers, nurses, doctors, industrial psychologists, army officers and many others to use counselling skills in a context-appropriate way. Many professions have codes of ethics and practice (some statutory) which, whilst they do not preclude the use of counselling skills, have elements which may be at variance with counselling values and ethics. In an attempt to conform to two different sets of values and codes of ethics, many competent practitioners are terminally de-skilled by role-conflict. The problem is avoided if the practitioner can feel securely labelled as a "*counsellor*" or a "nurse/teacher/priest *using counselling skills*".

As far as the counselling/therapy profession is concerned, there are several professional bodies representing therapists with various theoretical approaches, all of which have their own codes of ethics and practice. The BAC code covers such issues as responsibility to the client and to the wider community, counsellor competence, confidentiality and advertising practice. Copies of both BAC Codes can be obtained from BAC at the address given in the Appendix.

3. Telephone Counselling
When starting out to write this book I thought for a long time about the title. I wasn't sure whether it should be called 'Telephone Counselling Skills', or 'Using Counselling Skills on the Telephone". You will now appreciate some of the issues lying behind my decision.

The fact that I decided on the latter (and given my opinions expressed above) should, I hope, leave you in no doubt that I favour a strong differentiation between 'Counselling' and 'Using Counselling Skills'. In the case of telephone work we need to decide whether we are 'telephone counsellors' or 'using counselling skills on the telephone'. For the purpose of this Guide, I am taking the view that we are using counselling skills on the telephone. This then includes any telephone helping activity eg. listening, advising, information giving, tutoring etc. including counselling itself. I believe that using counselling skills on the telephone will help in all of these activities and a few more besides.

Before we try to define telephone counselling, the first question to answer is not "What is it?", but "Can it be done?" In order to answer this question we need to discover whether there is anything implicit in the definitions of counselling which requires that counselling be done face-to-face. A not-very-thorough literature search reveals that there is no just cause or impediment to stop '*telephone*' and '*counselling*' being joined in holy matrimony. That does not mean, however, that the provision of a good counselling relationship over the telephone is easy. Counselling in any setting is difficult, and whilst the telephone provides a different set of challenges from working face-to-face it is probably no more difficult. Some of these points have been addressed more fully in Chapter 1, others will be looked at elsewhere in this book. In summary, the main differences relate to:

> i) the quality of psychological contact between the counsellor and client,

> ii) the effect of the telephone on boundary issues,

> iii) the emphasis on the implementation of certain counselling skills,

> iv) the effect of the telephone on the counsellor's ability to discharge their ethical and professional responsibilities.

So, if telephone counselling can be done, is it sufficient to define it as 'Doing counselling on the telephone'? My guess is that this definition is perfectly adequate as long as we don't fall into the trap of thinking that '*on the telephone*' simply means '*out of sight*'. The telephone changes the relationship dynamics in many more ways than just preventing visual contact.

4. Using Counselling Skills on the Telephone

As each activity is successively outlined, those remaining become easier to see and identify. Having tied down the differences between 'counselling' and 'counselling skills' it should be a simple matter to put '*using counselling skills*' and '*working on the telephone*' together. If the use of counselling skills is not limited to counsellors, then many professionals (nurses, teachers, youth workers etc) should not only be able to use counselling skills but also offer them in their work over the phone. The kinds of telephone activities which will be improved by counselling skills include listening, information giving, advising, guiding, and tutoring. This covers services offered by organisations from Samaritans to the Open University, and activities performed by all kinds of designated workers from telephone receptionists through telephone helpline volunteers to distance learning tutors.

Unless your job includes deliberately inflicting pain on people, the addition of counselling skills never degrades any people-related activity. Counselling skills always improve communication and facilitate clearer mutual respect and understanding.

What Kind of Setting?

If a definition of an activity is not complete without identifying the setting in which it is practised, we need to look briefly at the kind of settings in which telephone counselling skills might be offered. **Firstly** there are open-access services not requiring specialist referral:

> • Where genuine telephone counselling is offered either as a stand-alone service or in association with a face-to-face service eg Open Door, Birmingham.

> • Drop-in generic or thematic counselling services where the telephone is the first point of contact or an appointment making device eg Relate or some Victim Support services.

> • Generic 'listening' services eg Samaritans.

> • Thematic information, advice and guidance services either telephone only or in association with a walk-in service eg Youth Access agencies or Welfare Rights services.

> • Thematic Helplines eg Childline, Aidsline.

Secondly there is a range of agencies and services operated by the health or social services which mostly require specialist referral - GP, social worker or other professional. Such services include:

Community Health Teams eg Alcohol, Drugs or Mental Health.

Specialist Health Services eg Genetic Counselling, Amputee Counselling.

Thirdly are the few individuals who offer a telephone counselling service as a specialism. This may be as a supplemental support for face-to-face work with disabled people for example or as a telephone-only service in a remote rural location.

Lastly are the 'others', a catch-all bag in which I would include welfare departments in large firms, Open University tutors, Psychiatric Day-Hospitals, and so on.

In all of these settings, I can think of no group of people whose performance would not be improved by counselling skills, and if they do telephone work, an appreciation of how to use counselling skills on the telephone. This book will speak directly to those whose job it is to deal with people in distress on the telephone. Some sections will be of more use to those people working for an agency, some sections will be more useful for those just starting out on training.

3 Before the Call

Getting ready to start telephone counselling is rather like going on holiday or making a long car journey - careful preparation makes all the difference between a successful event and possible disaster. You would not think of making a long car journey without :

* checking the mechanical condition of the car,
* filling up with petrol,
* making sure you have enough qualified drivers,
* correct insurance and
* a map.

Having such a checklist for counselling is, in essence, no different whether we are counselling on the telephone or face-to-face , but our pre-counselling checklist will be somewhat different. For telephone work, my checklist is divided into two sections:

i) The agency checklist (things an agency must do to provide an effective service and to protect its workers/volunteers and clients).

ii) The individual counsellor's checklist (things you and I must do as counsellors to ensure we and our clients are safe enabling us to work to our full potential).

There are two reasons why I include the agency checklist in a book meant for individual counsellors. Firstly, very few people do telephone counselling on their own. Most people belong to some telephone counselling organisation either as a paid worker or unpaid volunteer. *You should not compromise on your standards if you are a volunteer. Make your requirements known and stick to them if you value the quality of your work.*

The second reason is clear - for your own protection and the safety of your clients, think hard about working in an agency which does not provide the basic facilities and services on the checklist. Would you travel in a car without an MOT or with an unqualified driver without insurance?

Agency Checklist:

Agency Policy - is there one?

If Yes does it cover:
•Training
•Support and supervision

•Boundaries
•Advertising
•Worker/volunteer personal safety
•Equal opportunities for workers & clients
•Legal issues
•Insurance
•Abusive calls

•Referrals

•Silent calls

Are there enough workers/ volunteers?
Does the rota system work?
Are the premises adequate?
Is the telephone system adequate and appropriate for the service?
For how long is funding secure?

Personal Checklist:

Do you feel properly supported on the following issues by the agency:
•Sufficient Training
•Adequate support & supervision
•Boundaries
•Congruent advertising
•Your personal safety
•Countering discrimination

•Understanding the law
•Are you insured?
•Do you have to listen to abuse? Are you allowed to put the phone down on abusive callers?
•Who do you take referrals from and make them to?
•Are you allowed end silent calls?

Do you feel personally able to take on this work today?
Have you left your personal issues behind?
Are you familiar with the agency routines?

Well, how did you and your agency do? Don't worry if you didn't understand some of the issues - this chapter will be explaining each of them in turn and giving some recommendations for good practice where appropriate. Also don't worry if you or your agency fail to come up to scratch; you both have to start somewhere.

Only worry if you have identified a shortfall but neither you nor your agency want to do anything about it.

The checklist above may not be exhaustive. I'm sure readers can add to it and I'm equally sure some agencies will not like having some of these issues raised in this way. At least the debate can now begin.

> In Training : try getting trainees to make up their own pre-counselling safety checklists. Not only does it highlight issues for them, it may well give you clues as to how well your agency meets acceptable standards of practice.

Personal Checklist: Agency Policy
The first question on the Personal Checklist implies that

i) there is an agency policy (however adequate) and
ii) that you know about it and what it says.

Your first task is to find out whether there is one and track down a copy to check it out.

Every agency offering counselling, advice or guidance of any description should have a policy covering the issues on the checklist. I cannot emphasise this strongly enough. A good policy creates a sound structure or framework within which you can safely work with your clients. It is, if you like, the agency's way of creating the **core conditions for** *providing* **counselling** (see Chapter 4) within which you, the counsellor can be effective. You could say that an agency policy covering the points above is **necessary but not sufficient** (see Chapter 4) for an effective service.

An agency without a policy will fail to provide safe working environment for its counsellors and clients. If counsellors do not have sound guidelines on confidentiality and referrals, adequate support and supervision, sufficient training or work in an agency that doesn't have a clear idea about the work that it does, then they cannot give 100% of their attention to their clients.

For counselling to be successful the counsellor must give full attention to the client, confident in the knowledge that the agency is holding the safety net woven from the elements listed above. Counsellors should do the counselling and the agency should take care of the rest. Let's see how this might work out in practice. Because this book is aimed at individual counsellors, I will tackle the points on the *Personal Checklist* and, where appropriate, make reference to agency policy as I go.

Training and Supervision
If I had to pick two elements which are absolutely essential to the running of any counselling agency, they would be training and supervision. It is no accident, then, that you find them at the top of both the personal and agency checklists.

Training and supervision share certain features:

* All professional counsellors acknowledge them as essential re-quirements for effective, responsible counselling practice.
* They are both required by the British Association for Counselling before we can become Accredited Counsellors.
* Both are ongoing processes. Neither can ever be said to be finished or complete.
* Successful counsellors are not only committed to ongoing per-sonal and professional development through training and super-vision, they positively relish both.
* You should not call what you are doing 'counselling' unless you are

properly trained and adequately supervised.

* Agencies should not offer 'counselling' unless the staff are properly trained and adequately supervised.

Supervision will be covered in Chapter 7, so for now I will concentrate on training.

Training

As a freelance trainer I am often asked to run a weekend session on counselling skills, after which the participants are expected by their employers to demonstrate their new-found proficiency on the poor, unsuspecting public. In a similar vein, people expect to become proficient in counselling after completing a ten week evening class. I mention these examples in particular because most telephone counselling agencies think this is enough.

It is not enough. Whilst any training is probably better than none, we must be careful to not overestimate what can be achieved in a short time period and in my experience, some training does prove that the old saying "a little knowledge is dangerous" can sometimes be true.

So how much is enough? There have been various recommendations regarding the length of training required to equip the average person with sufficient skills to do various types of counselling. I will cut a long story very short and add my own views for good measure. Current thinking suggests that a course needs to have at least 100 hours 'contact' in order to train people to use *counselling skills*. Many college evening classes are around this length - it represents one evening a week for an academic year. A course of over 400 hours 'contact' is recommended to train *counsellors*. Good reference points here are the BAC Courses Recognition Scheme and Relate training. Both aim to train counsellors, not counselling skills.

A further question relates to the period of time should these contact hours should occur. Should they be done in one block or over a certain number of weeks? Here personal and/or agency circumstances will suggest particular patterns. Some people believe that learning counselling takes a while. The changes in attitudes and development of skills required can take some time to 'ferment', like good wine. Certain flavours can't develop overnight; they need a certain amount of ageing. It may be that the best results are obtained when training lets this consolidation of learning take place at a more 'natural' pace rather than put it in the pressure cooker environment of an intensive training programme. If you are making a big investment in training it may be more important to get the best trainers possible and choose a course timetable that your workers can most comfortably manage.

Lastly, the size of the training group is very important. It is clearly impossible to 'teach' counselling skills to a group of thirty people. The process requires close attention to each group member and good feedback to each individual. How many trainees can a good trainer give such attention to at any one time? Many trainers work in pairs (this is good practice and some accrediting bodies require it), but a trainer-trainee ratio of 1 to 15 for theory, 1 to 12 for personal development and 1 to 10 for skills is about right. Smaller groups are an improvement, larger groups degrade the training experience.

What should good training consist of? A good counsellor is 'well rounded'. That is to say that they have a good grasp of the **theory** of counselling, they can demonstrate good counselling **skills** and they have a reasonably high degree of self-awareness, gained from **personal development**. A further ingredient is that the first three components must be **congruent**. In other words, the theory, skills and personal work must be in accord, drawn from the same general approach or if drawn from many sources (eclectic), integrated in a logical, thoughtful and meaningful way.

The above four components of a counsellor must be represented in training. Training should have a good balance between theory, skills and personal work, and be congruent.

Theory

In one sense, theory is easy enough to find, since there are plenty of good books available. I have listed some of my favourites in the Appendix. However, a good trainer is required to help present the theory so that it can be translated into effective practice. That is where skills training comes in.

Skills

Learning to do counselling can be compared to learning how to drive a car:

* You need practical experience built in to the learning process. It is not enough to know the theory of driving, you have to practice the skills of driving as well.

Knowing counselling theory is not enough. Counselling is a skills-based activity and can not be developed just by reading books.

* You need to get practical experience in a gradual way, first in the safety of a dual control vehicle under the watchful eye of an approved instructor, moving on to practice in between lessons with the instructor by going out into the traffic with a friend or relative who has already passed their test.

Developing counselling skills is best done in as near to a 'real' counselling setting as possible. Training courses must build in this kind of activity in. Role playing is only good enough for very simple exercises. There is no substitute for real counselling.

* When learning to drive a car you are exposed to almost every type of traffic situation.

If possible, training should provide varied experiences of counselling including opportunities for the development of skills appropriate for ongoing counselling. Some training courses only offer opportunities to practice the initial interview over and over again.

Chapter 4 looks at counselling skills and how they can be put into practice on the telephone but as I have pointed out, I don't believe that reading this book will be enough. That's why it's called **'An**

Incomplete Guide'. What's missing is you and your experience, particularly your counselling skills practice. This can only be developed in relationships with others and these training relationships with your peers are the pivot around which your developing counselling skills turn. Not only do these relationships give you a 'safe' arena in which to practise your budding skills, they also give you the opportunity to receive good feedback and finally they give you and your fellow trainees the opportunity to be a client in counselling. (More on this in a moment.) Don't worry if your skills aren't tip-top, you'll get better and your colleagues will know that in this training relationship you'll be taking risks and using them as 'guinea pigs'. Don't put up with training that only offers role-plays.

Personal Development
Some people think that this is the most important ingredient in training, to the extent that they believe that people become good enough counsellors after an extended period of personal therapy or group work. I don't share that particular view, but I would not recommend any training that didn't make a firm commitment to personal work in some shape or form. Personal development is important for a number of reasons. Our self awareness can be 'mapped out' using a *johari window*:

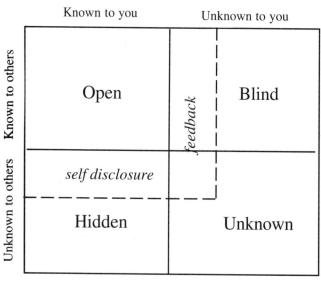

For those unfamiliar with this diagram, the open area is your conscious, open behaviour, known to you and others. The blind area is where others can see things about you that you cannot see yourself. The hidden area represents things we know about ourselves which we do not reveal to others. The unknown area includes feelings and motivations within you but unknown to both yourself and others. You know it's there because from time to time some of these aspects of yourself become known, and then you realise that these previously unknown feelings have been influencing your behaviour all along.

When I say that counsellors need to be self-aware, I mean that through ongoing self development (including opportunities available in counselling skills training) we seek to expand the 'Open' area in the *johari window*. This is achieved in personal development by two complimentary processes,

> i) receiving *feedback* from others and
> ii) by talking about ourselves honestly as we can, or *self-disclosure*.

Those using counselling skills on the telephone:

> • need to be sufficiently emotionally stable and self aware to be able to respond well to the emotional content of calls;
>
> • should not use the service or callers to meet their own emotional needs;
>
> • should be able to work as a member of a team if working in an agency;
>
> • should know their own skill and emotional limitations;
>
> • should be open and able to accept feedback and incorporate suggestions into new ways of being;

• should be actively committed to counselling as an acceptable agent for positive change and growth.

Anyone who will not participate in the personal development activities in a counselling skills training programme cannot be assured of meeting these criteria. In particular, they will not have demonstrated their basic *faith* in the counselling process (the last criterion) since the best evidence of such faith would be for them to submit to the process as a client or participant in self development. Would you go to a dentist who was afraid to visit the dentist her/ himself or thought that they somehow didn't need to go? Such a dentist would be a poor prospect indeed and I would worry about their sensitivity to my anxieties about dentists and their appreciation of the pain I might feel if they have never been in the dentist' chair themselves.

When asked to participate as a client in a real counselling session in a training situation, I sometimes hear trainees say "But I haven't got any problems or anything to talk about. I'd rather make something up." My experience is that everyone has something to talk about - a difficult decision, something mildly upsetting that happened at home or work, something that they saw on television that got to them on an emotional level, and so on. The counselling sessions in training need not be packed with world shattering problems from the depth of your soul and can remain confidential if necessary.

Boundaries
When I first heard the word 'boundaries', it didn't take long for me to realise that although I hadn't used the word in this context before, I was all too familiar with the concepts. I suppose in common parlance the closest single word that explains 'boundaries' is the word 'rules', but counsellors would never use the word '*rules*'! The term 'boundaries' is more figurative than 'rules' since it indicates an enclosed space; sacred space, safe space, open space, the client's space, space in which to grow. In order to give the counselling space these qualities, we need to protect it with boundaries. These boundaries will keep certain worldly things out and certain counsel-

ling values in, for example:

Out:	sexual contact	**in**:	empathy
	other exploitation		warmth
	gossip		confidentiality
	hierarchy		genuineness

A good list of boundaries can be found in the BAC Codes of Ethics and Practice. (Although they are not called boundaries in these publications.) There are different ones for Counsellors, Counselling Skills, Trainers and Supervisors. Your agency should have copies of all those available, if not, copies are available from BAC at the address given in the Appendix.

In Training : Split the group and ask what features they would require in order to create a safe/secure/ sacred space for themselves. Share and discuss. How close are these to BAC Codes?

Then do the same exercise but this time for safe/ secure telephone relationships.
How closely does this match with agency policy?

So what boundary issues are of particular importance in telephone relationships? To some extent this depends upon the agency you work for, since the service it is offering will determine sensible boundaries. Clearly some boundaries will be more important than others.

Tick off the important ones for you and your agency in the following list:
*Confidentiality.
*Counsellor anonymity.
*Gifts/payment from clients.
*When should a counsellor not accept a particular caller

client?
*Counselling friends/acquaintances or becoming friends with clients.
*Sexual contact with clients.
*Counselling clients of other helping agencies.
*Is face-to-face contact permitted, prohibited or encouraged?
*Who can end calls - counsellor or client only?

Each issue in the list above needs careful consideration by agencies offering telephone services. We will look at the importance of knowing where your agency stands in relation to each one in the section on Congruent Advertising. For the moment, I will highlight the boundary issue which occurs in all counselling settings and has a slightly different emphasis for telephone work: confidentiality.

'Confidentiality' and 'Privacy' are different.
On the phone it's important to distinguish between these two features of the counselling boundary. This problem would not occur in a face-to-face setting since it would be assumed that the interview was private, ie that no-one else is present.

Confidentiality refers to the treatment of information disclosed to you by the client, including their identity.

Privacy refers to the setting in which the counselling takes place. A setting can be somewhere on a sliding scale between private or public.

Some public settings can be confidential - sitting on a park bench with no-one else in hearing range. Some private interviews are not confidential. Privacy is a condition which can be infringed at either end of the phone - the client may be phoning from a public telephone or may have someone else in the room with him/her, and the counsellor may have other counsellors in the same room when the call is being received. Such infringements of privacy are often detectable by both counsellor and client. It is important that the counsellor doesn't make claims for the counselling that can't be guaranteed. Don't say the agency provides a private and confidential service if you can guarantee only one condition or neither.

Privacy

Clients might expect their call to be received in private and confidential surroundings, regardless of what your publicity says. Although I've never seen any agency which says - "All calls are confidential but not private". How would your client feel if after hearing your assurances that the call is confidential, they could hear other voices in the background (a common experience for callers to helplines) or a voice saying "Hey, Pete, would you like a cup of coffee?"

At the client's end, privacy could be disturbed by someone coming into the room. This can often be signalled by changes in the client's behaviour such as giving one word answers, hesitations and pauses in mid-sentence, losing track of ideas etc. If this happens, say to your client

> "It sounds as if someone has walked in on you. If they have, just answer, 'Yes'."

You can then either ride out the intrusion or move to a swift reassuring close using 'Yes'/'No' answers from your client. In some cases a client will just hang up without warning to protect their privacy.

It is important that you feel supported by agency policy and office rules as far as privacy and noisy surroundings are concerned. Agency policy may say:

> Counselling calls **will** be taken in private.
> Closed doors **will** be respected.
> **No** talking in the office when a call is taken.
> Extension phones **must not** be left plugged in.
> Eavesdropping is **not** allowed.

Confidentiality

Keeping information disclosed by clients confidential is a major factor in establishing an environment in which your clients can feel safe and secure. In order to avoid confusion amongst agency workers and to protect counsellors, there should be an agency policy on confidentiality. You may even like to consider asking every worker to sign a written statement on confidentiality as part of your recruitment procedure.

Agency policy should be:
   • clearly written;
   • available to all workers, not just counsellors;
   • made known to all callers at appropriate times during their helping relationship;
   • fully explained in training and induction to all agency workers.

Agency policy should cover:
   • what categories of information are confidential;
   • under what circumstances and to whom confidential information would be disclosed;
   • lines of support in confidentiality disputes;
   • who has the final say in matters of disclosure of information - client, counsellor, supervisor, manager?
   • the legal position on confidential records.

Examples of agency statements on confidentiality:
   • confidentiality is not kept just between the individual worker and client. Confidentiality is shared between past, present and future workers;
   • do not speak about callers when off duty, even when you think the caller cannot be identified;
   • only talk about callers to other agency workers when on duty, always protect their identity. Always have a reason to talk about a caller (eg supervision or support), never gossip;
   • never break confidence without the client's know-

ledge;
* always seek the client's permission before speaking to a third party;
* only the agency manager may speak to anyone outside the agency eg police, social services, GP's etc.

The legal position

As far as the legal situation is concerned, the law is constantly changing in two respects. Firstly, the various laws concerning confidential information are occasionally re-written. And secondly, as cases are tried in Court, certain judgements set legal precedents. Therefore, anything written here, today, may well be out of date by the time you read it. Agencies should seek legal advice before writing their policy on confidentiality to ensure maximum protection for both their staff and their clients.

In general, agencies and individuals do not have to disclose information to the police or anyone else for that matter (there are two exceptions - see below) even when the information concerns crimes as serious as murder. You will not commit an offence by withholding information asked for unless,
i) it relates to the Prevention of Terrorism Act, when withholding information without reasonable excuse is an offence, and
ii) you are ordered by a court to produce information and you refuse, in which case you may be in contempt of court and may be fined or imprisoned.

If you ever tangle with the law, seek legal advice immediately and don't give any information unless advised to do so. Even then it's up to you. Your legal adviser will tell you the probable consequences of withholding information.

Some agencies may keep information on a computer. Whether this is information on clients, staff, sponsors or any other individuals, you may have to register under the Data Protection Act. Again seek advice from a legal expert or the Data Protection Act Registrar's office.

Advertising

Publicity and promotional material needs to not only 'sell' your service, it also has to be congruent. By this I don't mean that the advertising has to be simply honest in its portrayal of the service you are offering - although this is absolutely essential if you are to establish and maintain credibility. It has to be 'in the manner of' your agency in the way it portrays your mission, aims and objectives. This is because the advertising you produce may be the first point of contact a person has with your service and your potential clients are already forming opinions about what kind of people you are and what it might be like to ask you for help as a result of this publicity material. In short this material is the first part of the process whereby you **structure** your helping relationship with your clients.

[A brief word about structuring:

Structuring is the process whereby the client and counsellor draw up the 'rules' of the relationship. This happens in an unspoken way in all 'relationship episodes', however brief.

When you walk down the street and see an acquaintance approach, both of you quickly negotiate by means of a series of rapid glances and bodily movements. By the time you meet, you will have decided how long you are prepared to have a meeting for, roughly what the meeting will be about and how intimate you will be with each other. Will you warmly greet each other and embrace or say a quick 'Hello' and pass by? If one of you gets it wrong, there will be an embarrassing and awkward moment.

We align our expectations of each relationship episode every time we meet someone and we know all too painfully what happens when one of us gets it wrong.

We will see in Chapter 4 how to structure your relationship with the client when they start a counselling relationship, ie when the first telephone interview starts. However, the process of structuring your relationship with the client started long before that. It started the moment there was any contact between the agency and the client. It was at that moment that the client started to build expectations about any future relationship s/he might have with you:

> **Is the agency organised and reliable or slapdash?*
> **Will the counsellors be warm and friendly or cold and authoritarian?*
> **Are the helpers 'expert advisers' or 'equal partners' in the helping process?*
> **Do the counsellors listen to the clients or tell the clients what to do?*
> **Will clients behaviour be judged?*
> **Is the service confidential - can it be trusted?*

*Does your publicity lead your potential clients to have an accurate idea of what your agency is like. It it **congruent**?*

The process of structuring continues if the reader of your publicity decides to call your agency or pay a visit to your premises. What do they find on first contact? What does the voice on the phone or the entrance to your building tell them?

> **Is the agency organised and reliable or slapdash?*
> **Will the counsellors be warm and friendly or cold and authoritarian?*
> **Are the helpers 'expert advisers' or 'equal partners' in the helping process?*
> **Do the counsellors listen to the clients or tell the clients what to do?*
> **Will clients behaviour be judged?*
> **Is the service confidential - can it be trusted?*

And so it goes on - reception areas, reception staff, manner of greeting; you name it. Everything that happens to a potential client is helping them decide what you're like and whether they want to be helped by you. The publicity material you use should not try to 'sell' your agency, but help clients align their expectations so that they will not be disappointed or disoriented when they finally arrive in *the counselling session - whether on the phone or face to face. Your publicity should be **congruent**.*]

Given the need for congruence in publicity, here is a checklist to help you assess the image you are getting across:

Agency name: •Are you happy that the agency name gives the right impression?
•Does your logo give an accurate impression of the values and mission of the agency?

Publicity: •Is it clear about the kind, range and availability of services you offer?
•Does it give a realistic picture and not raise false expectations - eg have you the staff and re- sources to deliver what you claim?

Distribution: •Do you place publicity where it will reach as wide a range of potential clients as possible?
•Have you identified potential client groups, what they read and where they meet?
•Do you use a wide range of media?
•Do you exploit free publicity, eg local press editorials etc?
•Do you give talks to interested organisations and those which represent your potential client groups?

Personal Safety
All organisations must have a concern for the safety of their staff. This will be particularly true of organisations which require people to work in the evenings or at night. You must decide when and where you feel most vulnerable and ask your agency for protection. If you're not sure what this might mean, here are some ideas:

Counsellor anonymity - in addition to protecting the identity of your callers, you may well expect your privacy to be respected too.

Is there an agency policy which says that your personal details must not be given to anyone without your permission, and never to a client even with your permission?

Getting home - if you are expected to work shifts that begin or end at night, are you given a lift or escorted home or to a place of safety?

At the office - does agency policy say that no-one must be in the office alone? Are there panic buttons located in all rooms where you might meet clients or strangers on your own? Do you feel secure when you are on duty?

> In Training : Suggest a mini counselling session (15 minutes each way) on personal safety. Split group into pairs to explore their feelings on the issue. Share in the large group and be aware that some people may have had distressing personal experiences.

The issue of personal safety is not simply about ensuring your physical safety, but also about ensuring that you *feel* safe whilst working. You can hardly be expected to create a safe secure space for your clients if you do not feel safe and secure yourself. Your feelings of insecurity will be detected by clients and may well rub off on them. Make sure that your need for a safe working environment doesn't turn your agency premises into a prison. You need to feel comfortable too!

Equal Opportunities
It should go without saying in 1993 that every public service agency should have an equal opportunities policy. In telephone counselling it is particularly important because whilst we may be trying to be available to all client groups, it has been found that black people, disabled people and males particularly from working class backgrounds are under-represented in counselling. Your agency should

ensure that there is at least equal access to:
- •recruitment procedures and training - for potential staff
- •agency services - for clients
- •premises - both clients and staff
- •publicity - is it distributed in places accessible to disabled people, for example?

This is achieved by:
i) careful preparation and monitoring of publicity and recruit ment procedures;
ii) deliberate focusing on issues of oppression and equal opportunities in training; and
iii) careful attention to developing non-discriminatory office procedures.

> In Training : Ensure that equal opportunities issues are given a high profile. Ask the group what they think the needs of oppressed groups might be as far as your service is concerned. Collate views on flipchart discuss and compare to agency policy.
> Pay careful attention to racist or sexist attitudes and language used by trainees.

Some agencies will have policies designed to make themselves particularly user-friendly to some oppressed groups by having, eg special disabled access, a large number of black counsellors etc. Other agencies will prefer to make access easier still for certain oppressed groups by designating themselves a specialist service eg women only, gay advice line, etc. Make sure your agency publicity carries an equal opportunities or anti-oppression statement. Don't work for the agency if you don't agree with its position on equal opportunities.

Insurance
It is increasingly important that agencies and their workers enjoy

proper protection through appropriate insurance cover. This is easy to arrange through an insurance broker for public liability (if your chimney pot falls on the head of a passer by) and BAC will give advice on professional liability (if a client claims s/he was damaged by your advice, guidance or counselling).

Abusive calls and silent calls
The skills required to deal with these types of call are dealt with in Chapter 4. Here we are attending to the issue of whether your agency has a policy which clearly explains your responsibilities to the caller and the agencies responsibilities to you.

For example:
- who can end a call?
- are you allowed to put the phone down, or must you always wait for the client to do so?
- how long must you wait in silence before deciding to put the phone down on a caller?
- must you listen to an abusive or threatening caller?
- does your agency have anything to say about 'hoax' calls ie:
  What are they?
  Who defines them?
  How can you recognise one?
  What do you do when you think you've got one?
- who is your first line of support should you receive a difficult call?

In Training : Make the issue of abusive or threatening calls the subject of a mini counselling session. Split the group into pairs and ask them to help each other explore their feelings about abusive, threatening and silent calls. Share in large group.

Every agency policy should create a secure space in which you can offer a helping relationship to the callers. It is the agency's way of providing the core conditions necessary for the provision of a good telephone counselling relationship. If you are unsure how to act in any set of circumstances, your first stop is your agency policy. If that doesn't help you should *act in the way which feels right for you* and seek support as soon as the call or situation is over. The same goes for the next section.

Referrals

To feel completely supported by an agency policy it should tell us what the limits of the agency service are. This includes helping us decide who we should accept referrals from and to whom we may refer clients and under what circumstances. Along with agency guidelines on referral we should also have a keen sense of our own limits of competence and our personal emotional limits. How and to whom do we refer when we think we can't help or can't cope.

To help with basic referral strategy, the agency should provide a list of approved referral routes into and out of the agency. You should also feel that you have the skills (developed in training) to receive a referral with confidence and refer a client on without leaving the client feeling 'difficult', rejected or unworthy.

Today's duty - are you ready?

I started off this chapter by comparing preparing for telephone counselling with preparing to go on a long car journey. So far we've done the equivalent of checking that the car is road worthy and that we are properly qualified and insured to drive.

What about personal 'here-and-now' checking?
> Have you been drinking alcohol?
> Have you had a sensible meal?
> Do you feel tired?
> Do you want to go to the toilet?
> Are you dressed sensibly?

We would do all of these things automatically before driving a long distance, and generally speaking I wouldn't start a counselling duty if I didn't think I was fit to drive. The same kind of checks apply, because I need to feel physically and emotionally capable of doing the job. Both driving and counselling are very responsible activities. Lives can be at stake, so I try to make sure I'm in a fit state to do the job.

In particular, counsellors need to be sure that they are emotionally capable of providing a supportive relationship on any given day. Sometimes it isn't possible, since fate has a habit of throwing up unexpected events in everyone's life - counsellors included. Family illness, bereavement, unemployment, any sort of bad news can cast doubt on your capacity to help others. And it needn't be just bad news which can throw you off track - I pity the poor client who is counselled by me just after I'm told that I've won a million on the pools! The point is, only I can really tell how I feel, and I must responsibly ask myself before each duty whether I can be a good enough counsellor.

Most days are neither desperately bad nor fantastically good. They are firmly stuck in that grey area in between - could be better, could be worse. Usually my task is to make sure that I can leave issues in my personal life behind. I don't want to visit them on my clients. They're coming to 'me' for help.

It is nice to feel supported by agency policy, fellow counsellors and agency management. To know that if I say, "No, I can't do it today", they will understand that I have my own and the client's best interests at the centre of my actions.

4 On The Telephone

In Chapter 2, I took some time to explain why it is so important to define the activity and why I decided to use the title 'Using Counselling Skills on the Telephone'. What follows in the current chapter is my best effort to describe the interaction between counselling skills and the telephone. As I wrote, again in Chapter 2, there is no reason why 'Telephone Counselling' in the therapeutic sense of the word can't be offered by a properly qualified and supervised person, however the skills I will refer to in this chapter are not in themselves sufficient to offer 'Telephone Counselling'.

In Chapter 3, I ran through the reasons why good training is important and what training would be appropriate for those who wish to offer counselling skills. Reading this chapter and trying out the ideas in isolation, in the absence of a trainer, is similarly insufficient preparation for offering counselling skills on the telephone.

The idea is that this chapter, indeed the whole book, should supplement your experience either as a user of counselling skills on the phone or in your training and preparation for that work.

'Core' Counselling Conditions
In 1957 Carl Rogers wrote an article in which he argued that certain conditions need to be in place before any helping activity can be effective. He wrote that there are six 'core conditions' for therapeutic change and that these conditions must exist and continue over a period of time:

1 Two persons are in psychological contact.

2 The first, the client, is in a vulnerable or anxious state.

3 The second person, the therapist (counsellor) is congruent or integrated (genuine) in the relationship.

4 The counsellor experiences unconditional positive regard (acceptance) for the client.

5 The counsellor experiences empathic understanding of the client's world and viewpoint, and tries to communicate this to the client.

6 The counsellor is able to communicate these conditions to the client to a minimal degree.

Whilst some of the words may sound like jargon, the gist of it is clear, and over the years we have come to think of three conditions (3, 4 and 5) as being the most obviously important. Much has been written about these three core conditions and a good understanding of them is an essential basis for sound effective counselling practice (whether on the telephone or face-to-face).

Before looking in a bit more detail at these three core conditions I want to focus on another one of Rogers' original six conditions which takes on a special importance when working on the 'phone. Number 1, which says that two persons must be in psychological contact in order for therapeutic change to take place.

Psychological Contact - What it is and how to maintain it on the telephone.

We take it for granted when sitting in the same room as our client, looking at them, making occasional eye contact with them, that we are in psychological contact with them. Take away that visual contact and suddenly we're not so sure.

On the telephone we have to make psychological contact and maintain it without the benefit of vision. In crude terms this means that we have to use our ears and our voice more in order to answer some fundamental questions:

• How do I find out if the caller is a client?

• How do I establish 'quality contact' with her/him?

If there is a pause in the conversation:

• How do I know the client is still there?

• How do I know the client still wants to talk?

• How do I know how comfortable the client feels?

• How does the client know I'm still here?

• How does the client know I'm still listening and interested?

Once I have established that the client is still there and that s/he knows that I am too, and since I can't see the client,

How long can I leave it before I need to check again?

In training : Split group into two's and three's and get them to answer these questions. Share answers large group and discuss.

In the **'Skills'** section later in this chapter we will look at some ways of answering these questions.

Empathy
Empathy is the effort of trying to see the world of another person

through their own eyes. It has been described as walking in someone else's shoes, understanding how someone else feels and thinks, sensitively entering into another person's private world of special meanings and so on.

Some books refer to 'accurate empathy' or 'empathic understanding'. I'm not sure that these words actually add to my understanding of empathy since I'm sure that inaccurate empathy would be of use to no-one, as indeed would empathic non-understanding. What we can say about empathy, however, is that it involves appreciating and understanding both the thoughts and the feelings of the client, both the content and the process, the 'words' and the 'music'.

Being empathic is what many refer to as 'active listening' and in face-to-face counselling that involves looking at the client as well as listening to them. In fact picking up clues any way you can as to what the client is thinking and how they are feeling. On the telephone you will be working with a restricted set of information, so you must learn to 'tune in' to the client by putting all of the sound-only clues to much better use than in the average face-to-face session.

Acceptance

Many clients come for counselling because they are afraid of being judged by others (maybe parents or friends) for something they have done or are planning to do. It is crucial that counsellors provide an atmosphere of total acceptance in which clients can feel free to explore their troubles without fear of being judged. American books often refer to this core condition as *unconditional positive regard*. Although this is a bit of a mouthful, its meaning can be made clear. The essence of it is that counsellors must see their clients as worthy (positive regard) regardless of what that person may have done (unconditional). Seeing someone as worthy does not mean that you have to approve of their behaviour or admire them. Simply see them as a human being of equal value.

Some British books call it *non-judgemental warmth*, another good term since it puts the rather neutral 'non-judgemental' bit next to the more positive 'warmth'. This also helps us break down the idea into two component skills - firstly the absence of judgement, secondly the communication of warmth. This core condition is not just the absence or suspension of judgement, but also the positive feeling of warmth towards the other person as a valuable worthy person. Many clients come for counselling in the first place because their feeling of worth has been damaged by painful experiences. By offering this core condition we can help heal those hurts.

Genuineness

Genuineness is the last of the three 'core' conditions written about by Carl Rogers. It involves the helper acting in a way that is honest, true to themselves, without front, mask or facade, without adopting a role such as 'expert' or 'teacher' and so on. Rogers described it as being 'transparently real' and includes being one's self in ways which may not be seen as ideal for counselling, for example, having 'negative' thoughts and feelings.

Within the core condition of genuineness lies a fundamental challenge to us all to be ourselves; fallible, vulnerable and even gullible, (see Chapter 5) complete with all manner of feelings. We must be our real self with our clients in a way which does not harm, diminish or take away from their own self worth. In this way they may come to see that it is safe to be themselves here in this session.

Rogers also said that these conditions were both necessary and sufficient.

Necessary : This means that therapeutic change will only take place if all three core conditions are present - if one is missing, change may take place but it will not be therapeutic. Of course there are many types of change - some positive and sought after, some negative and unhelpful. These 'core conditions' may be present in these situations to a lesser degree, but only when all three are there will the change be therapeutic.

Sufficient : If all three are present, even by accident, therapeutic change may take place even if it was not planned for. How many times have we found it really easy to talk over our problems and feel really helped in the most unlikely places? Also some people seem to be 'natural' listeners and find that others will seek them out to talk to. These are occasions when the core conditions are provided in an accidental, informal or unplanned way.

The core conditions are qualities rather than skills and other counsellors have tried to break down the core conditions and the therapeutic process in general into skills. The idea is to break down these qualities of helping into small enough parts to be able to understand them so that we can improve through repeated practice. This helps take the mystery out of providing a good quality helping relationship. The important ingredient needed to turn repeated practice into effective training is good quality, responsible **feedback**.

Skills

Rogers' ideas on the core conditions were developed by a number of writers including Gerard Egan (The Skilled Helper 1975 & 1882), who incorporated the three core conditions into a model in which Rogers' core conditions form the first of three stages. Many writers and trainers prefer to use Egan's three stage model to identify the skills required for therapeutic counselling.

Egan's three stage helping model.

Stage 1
Exploration: Creating a warm trusting relationship with the client, enabling the client to explore whatever they choose. Entering the client's 'frame of reference' (looking at the world from the client's point of view).
Skills: Active listening, communicating empathy, genuineness and non-judgemental warmth, acknowledging and reflecting feelings, paraphrasing, focusing and clarifying.

Stage 2
Understanding: Helping the client see their situation with new

understanding, from different perspectives, with alternative information.

Skills: All of Stage 1 skills plus summarising, linking and integrating issues into themes, offering new perspectives, sharing, challenging, immediacy (looking at what's happening right here and now between you and the client) and goal setting.

Stage 3
Action: Looking with the client at possible ways of acting in this situation. Assessing risks and possible outcomes. Helping the client evaluate the effectiveness of their new behaviour.
Skills: All of the skills of stages 1 & 2 plus brainstorming, creative thinking, planning, implementing and evaluating plans.

Many of these skills can be learned in a face-to-face context and transferred just as easily to a telephone context. So in the **majority** of cases there need be no special training as far as using counselling skills on the telephone is concerned but as I mentioned in Chapter 1, there are **some** special considerations to be made for telephone work. For those readers who have had little or no training, I will expand on each of these skills using telephone examples as I go. Wherever possible I will also give training suggestions.

There are two elements to all counselling skills - discrimination and communication. **Discrimination** is the picking up of the relevant information (from your client, yourself or any other source) and **communication** is the skill of letting your client know what information you've picked up. For example if the skill in question is active listening, there are two components - discrimination and communication. **Discrimination** is the listening part - not just to the words, but picking up all of the subtle nuances between the words, listening to the tone of voice, breathing patterns, trembling voice etc, trying to sense the feelings behind the story. **Communication** on the other hand, is the feeding back to your client that you have heard and understood what s/he is saying and feeling, checking that you are correct and indicating that it's the client's turn to talk.

The problems relating to maintaining psychological contact only arise when working on the phone. The establishment and maintenance of this contact requires high quality listening and a fair amount of talking from the counsellor.

Making Contact

In order to make contact and establish that you have a bona-fide client, most people have a comfortable telephone answering routine worked out. "Hello, Pete Sanders' Telephone Counselling Service here, can I help you?" or something similar will do. Don't worry if your opening lines begin to sound over-used, thousands of volunteers have been saying "Hello, Samaritans, can I help?" for well over 25 years without putting callers off.

Maintaining Contact

Once you have established that you have a bona-fide client rather than a wrong number, your next task is to keep in psychological contact with your client.

In face-to-face situations, this is made easier because you can use a number of sight-dependent actions such as
•looking at your client   •making eye contact
•smiling   •nodding your head
•leaning forward in your chair

On the 'phone we are restricted to maintaining this contact with verbal or sound-dependent methods only. When we can't see the person we are talking to, we become very sensitive to the way time passes in a conversation. Seconds seem like minutes and minutes seem to stretch on forever.

In Training : Split up into pairs and get one in each pair to close their eyes and guess when a minute of silence has elapsed. Or ask each pair start a conversation with their eyes closed and prime one person to lapse into silence after a minute or so.

> The second person then guesses when one minute
> has elapsed. Feedback and discuss.

This effect is not limited to counsellors. Clients feel it too; so we must work hard to keep contact with our clients so that they have a safe, secure atmosphere in which to receive the rest of our counselling skills. The only way to do this is to maintain our presence verbally by talking more and making more sounds in general than we would face-to-face. Typical ways to do this are by saying:

- Uh-huh
- Yes
- I see
- Right

- Mmm
- Please go on
- Do you want to say more about that?
- Ah-hah

These responses can be varied or combined ad infinitum eg: "Yes, please go on" or "Ah-hah, I see" etc.

Stage 1 Skills: Active listening and communicating empathy
Active listening is one of the key ingredients of empathy. It is not possible to be empathic if you are not actively listening. In face-to-face situations, active listening requires that you attend with your whole being to everything that the client is trying to communicate to you. That means using all of your senses, including sight. We get lots of information about the client and his/her feelings from the way they look and present themselves, their posture, their facial expressions, their gestures etc.

On the telephone we miss all of that and at the same time we get many vocal and breathing noises amplified above normal. This can be distracting. So on the phone we need to work a little bit harder to overcome the disadvantages of this restricted set of information. How can this be overcome? We must tune in to everything available to sense what the client is thinking and feeling. For example:

•Voice 'quality' - tone, pitch and volume. *Is it a strong or weak voice? Old or young? Confident or timid?*

•Breathing noises - sobbing, chattering teeth, sighing, holding their breath or crying. *Is the client sad, hurt, afraid or angry?*

•Speed of talking. *Is the client rushing and nervous or slow and relaxed? Speeding and excited or sluggish and depressed?*

•Other vocalisations such as laughter, snorting or grunting. *Is the client happy, sad, furious? Do they sound genuine?*

•Background noises. *Is the client alone or do they keep getting interrupted? How does this affect them?*

•Silence. *What is happening? Is the client pausing for thought?*

The other key ingredient in empathy is communication. It's no good me sitting on the end of the phone being the most empathic person in the world if I'm not communicating this to the client. The core conditions must be *experienced* by the client.

Reflection
The basic method of empathy is to reflect the content of the client's utterances back to them. By content I mean both the storyline content and the feelings content - this isn't necessarily spoken. (This is where all the jokes about counsellors nodding and saying "Uh huh, so you feel angry" after the client has just thrown the chair out of the window come from.)

In Training : It can help to start off by looking at feelings. Trainees can get hooked on getting the accuracy of the content of the client's story right at the expense of paying attention to the client's feelings. Putting the spotlight onto feeling early on can help stop this.

There are several ways to focus on feelings:
•Start by developing a vocabulary of feelings.
Split into twos, brainstorming as many feeling
words as possible. Share and collate in large
group. If someone doesn't understand a
particular word, get the person who
brainstormed it to explain.
•Use role plays to help trainees identify feelings
which they have problems hearing or
experiencing. (People that can't bear someone
else to be angry often have difficulty in
managing their own anger.)

The ability to give good reflections without sounding like a parrot is
simply a matter of making the activity natural to you. Don't judge the
art of reflection by your own wooden first attempts. That's a bit like
saying that ballroom dancing is just a matter of putting one foot after
another, trying it yourself for five minutes and then saying that it looks
stupid.

The real dancing starts when you can blend together technique and
natural self. Not only does it look as though the dancers are floating
effortlessly on air, it actually feels like that too! The same goes for
all counselling skills - reflecting in particular. When you get the hang
of it, it becomes an effortless second nature; not wooden at all. How
do you achieve this? The two ingredients of technique and natural self
must be brought together by a process of *practice* and *feedback*.

In Training : I have found it best to use a tape
recorder. In pairs, start off by recording
short snippets - say two minutes - of the start of a
counselling interview. Ask the counsellors to
concentrate on accurate reflection of the clients'
statements. Then play back and listen carefully to

the client's statements and the counsellor's responses. Is the counsellor's reflection accurate and complete? Move on to longer segments. Concentrate on getting the group to recognise complete and accurate reflection and giving good feedback to each other.

Then ask the group to give feedback on the individual qualities each counsellor brings to the art of reflection. As each counsellor gains confidence in their ability to be accurate on both a feelings and storyline level, emphasise the individual, natural qualities in the feedback.

Being empathic is quite difficult to start off with, and you may encounter some common problems. For example, many clients start off their first contact with a counsellor in a great rush with a torrent of words. They are understandably anxious and try to tell you their whole story in one block at the front end of the session. Your task is to be empathic, seeing the client's world from their point of view. Since the key skill is to communicate this understanding to the client and the basic method is reflection, the problem is how to actively listen, remember, accurately reflect and check for accuracy when the client won't stop talking to let you get a word in edgeways.

Many people believe that listening passively without doing anything other than saying "Yes", "I see", or "Uh huh", and nodding your head is enough. I do not believe it is. In the first place, we have to maintain contact with the client verbally on the phone and if they are talking all the time we can't do this. In the second place the key skill is *active* listening, not passive listening. This means encouraging the client to say more and reflecting the content of their statements so as to give the message:

"I'm listening to what you're saying and trying to understand. I will demonstrate this to you by letting you know that I heard what you just said. Here it is - have I got it right?"

The only way I have found to do this is to interrupt the client. Even when they are in full flow. This technique once mastered will enable you to break up the client's story into manageable chunks so that you can do a reasonable job of reflecting and communicating empathy.

You may worry that you client will be put off. You may worry that your client may lose the thread of their story. You may worry that your client will think you rude and disrespectful. It is my contention that you should interrupt in order to communicate the message:

> "What you are saying is so important that I must slow you down to make sure I catch it all."

This is a respectful thing to say. You can also try saying:

> "I realise that you want to tell me your story, but I can't keep up with you. Could you slow down a little and let me check every now and then to make sure I've got it right."

As well as enabling you to maintain contact, these interruptions will help you establish a pattern of *client statement - counsellor response*. This pattern will make any work on the telephone easier since the eye contact we normally use in order to manage a conversation is not available to us on the phone. When a comfortable *talk - listen - response* pattern is set up early in the interview, the client and counsellor can settle down to build up their relationship. Setting up this pattern is another example of **structuring** (see Chapter 3).

Structuring
Structuring is a way of aligning the client's expectations with what you are providing and when used to set up a pattern in this way, structuring will in itself communicate certain messages about the counselling relationship to the client:

•I (the counsellor) will listen and you (the client) will talk.

- You and your world are the centre of both this session and my complete attention.
- I am trying so hard to understand what you are thinking and feeling that I constantly check to make sure that I've got it right.
- I am not setting myself up as an expert.
- You are the expert on the subject of you.
- I am paying attention to both your story and your feelings.

If the client continues to talk too fast or for too long for you to grasp and reflect the key points, interrupt again. Try

> " I know I keep interrupting, but it's so important that I understand as much as possible."
> or
> "I realise you want to get this off your chest. That is why I'm interrupting you to make sure I've got it right."

If the client's flow is stopped, you will be aware of it, although in my experience this rarely happens - if a client really is bursting they can easily overcome a few interruptions. If the client is irritated or distracted by your interruptions, you will notice (sometimes they will tell you!). Again, this rarely happens in my experience but if it does try saying:

> "I can see that my interruptions are irritating you. If you could leave some gaps when you're talking, I can check to see if I'm understanding you correctly."

The 'technique' part of structuring is to
i) reflect what you see and hear
ii) be open and genuine and
iii) don't let the client get too far ahead of you by talking for too long otherwise you'll lose the thread.

The 'natural' part of structuring is achieved by practising until it becomes second nature. When I first sat in front of the wheel of a car and tried to drive off, I found it so difficult that I couldn't even begin to imagine how I could take my hands off the wheel to change gear, let alone look in the rear view mirror. After much practice I can now drive and turn on, and listen to, the radio or talk to the person sitting next to me, without even thinking about it. I am a confident, relaxed and natural driver and my driving style reflects my personality.

When learning a new skill we start off from a position of *unconscious incompetence* - we don't know which skills are needed nor do we know which skills we have or don't have. We move on to *conscious incompetence* when we start recognising the skills that we need but don't have. Next comes *conscious competence* where we have to concentrate like crazy in order to keep the skill going and doing it feels really awkward and artificial. Finally we arrive at *unconscious competence*, the 'radio-on-driving' I mentioned above or the "Look Ma, no hands!" stage. This is when an activity which once felt awkward, wooden and artificial, becomes second nature.

Paraphrasing, focusing and clarifying
These three skills are complementary to basic reflection and together with reflection form your 'empathy repertoire'. When used together they turn reflection from mere a parrotting of the client's words into a powerful method of communicating; your real effort to understand the client. This understanding can help the client move forward since you will be helping them clarify their often blurred and tangled issues.

Paraphrasing is the skill of summarising what the client is saying. This summarising can be of what the client has just said in their last utterance , what the client has been saying during the session, or even over several sessions. Paraphrasing the client's statements over a longer period may often reveal patterns in the client's issues which they may find helpful.

When paraphrasing it is sometimes best to use your own words and sometimes best to use the client's own words. Using the client's own words can sometimes capture a power that becomes diluted if you use your own. You must develop a sense of good judgement to know how best to paraphrase in any given situation.

Focusing is sensing the key issues in what the client is saying from the way the client is talking. Clients do sometimes say "This is the most important thing", but often they don't mean it and sometimes even when they do, their tone of voice gives a signal that something else is important too. Helping a client focus on the important issues is sometimes difficult on the phone because people have a tendency to ramble on over the phone, so you may have to develop your ability to interrupt to help your focusing. When you start out in counselling it's often good to be cautious or tentative when helping a client focus on the most important issues. Focusing is a skill which takes a fair degree of practice to get right, since if you get it wrong you may end up *telling* the client what's most important rather than *checking* with them that your hunch might be even vaguely right.

Clarifying is as self-explanatory as it sounds. It is the activity of helping your client to unravel a tangle, see clearly through a foggy patch, hear an inner whisper more distinctly. This involves accurate active listening and clear thinking on your part.

The three activities, summarising, focusing and clarifying when used with reflection to communicate with the client can build up to a powerful experience which in itself can enable clients to sort out problems. For some it is the end point of counselling. It can go something like this:

- Basic Reflection - Checking

  - Summarising - Reflection - Checking

    - Focusing - reflection - Checking

      - Clarification - Reflection - Checking

        - Solution - Reflection - Checking

Checking is simply checking that your reflections are accurately tracking the client's thoughts and feelings. Of course, the counselling process is not always this simple, but it can be occasionally, especially over the phone, since people often phone up with the expectation of getting things sorted in double-quick time. Strong expectations can turn into self fulfilling prophesies.

The final point about this 'empathy repertoire' is that in face-to-face counselling, new counsellors often feel that their brain is about to burst trying to listen to the client whilst remembering what they've just said, preparing a summary in their head, wondering what the key issues might be and then...oh no, it's gone! They've forgotten what the client's been saying. Here the phone comes into its own and delivers one of its great advantaged to you. You can make notes!

Making notes can be a boon when using the phone, but don't let it take over so that you can't pay attention to what your client is saying. Brief memory aids are fine, don't start taking verbatim notes or you'll find yourself muttering "Hang on, I haven't got that down yet!"

Communicating Genuineness

When it comes to genuineness or 'congruence' as Carl Rogers called it, many counselling texts offer a general description or definition of the activity from the client's point of view:

> "It has been found that personal change is facilitated when the psychotherapist is what he *is*, when in the relationship with his client he is genuine and without 'front' or facade, openly being the feelings and attitudes which at that moment are flowing *in* him."
> C Rogers (1967) On Becoming a Person, p 61. Constable.

Or from the counsellor's point of view:

> "I have come to recognise that being trustworthy does not demand that I be rigidly consistent but that I be dependably real. The term 'congruent' is one I have used to describe the way I

would like to be. By this I mean that whatever feeling or attitude I am experiencing would be matched by my awareness of that attitude. When this is true, then I am a unified or integrated person in that moment, and hence I can be whatever I deeply am."

C Rogers (1967) On Becoming a Person, p50. Constable.

Genuineness, then is any tangible expression of the counsellor's capacity to be in touch with her/his feelings, thoughts and bodily sensations as s/he seeks to understand the client's world of experience.

Moving from the general to the specific proves more difficult and examples are rarely quoted since the meaningful qualities of genuineness can only really be appreciated through personal experience. This is not a cop-out position since it is in the training situation where you will be provided with many moments which can be used by an experienced trainer to illustrate genuineness. In practice, genuineness raises itself as an issue in almost all counselling sessions.

The following are presented as thought provoking items, around which you might construct a better understanding of genuineness. How many of these statements do you worry about (or maybe you recognise some from your work with clients).

1   "What did the client say just then? I was distracted by that noise outside the window rather than paying attention to what she was saying."

2   "I don't like this person. How can I work with them when I don't like them?"

3   "I seem to be getting dragged into this person's problem and becoming part of it."

4   "I am so bored with this session, I can hardly keep my eyes open let alone my mind on what he's saying!"

5   "I feel manipulated by this client into saying something I don't want to say."

6   "I just can't understand what this client is talking about."

7   "Aha! The client has just described exactly what happened to me years ago. I remember feeling exactly the same!"

8   "Damn! She's hung up on me again. I get mad when she does that!"

9   "Oh dear, this seat is uncomfortable. I can't think straight my back is killing me!"

10   "Wow, I really fancy him/her!"

What should you do if you are stuck in one of these situations?

*Acknowledge the feelings you are having.

*Decide whether the feelings are roughly
    i) because of something in you (eg 1,2,9 or 10)
    ii) brought on by something the client has done/said (eg 5 or 8)
    iii) a mixture of your feelings and the client's behaviour
        (eg 4, 6 or 7)

*If you are fairly certain that the feelings are coming only from you then *don't act on them in the session.* You will need to talk to another person (your supervisor) about your feelings or emotional involvement in the client's problem. If it's a real burning issue, you may need some spot support from a colleague. (See Chapter 6). Number 9 is the exception here. If you are uncomfortable, get comfortable. You can usually do this without the client knowing when on the telephone. If you have to lose concentration for a moment, tell the client what you are doing:

> "I'm going to have to change this chair for a different one - it's so uncomfortable I can't pay proper attention to what you are saying."

*Not acting on your feelings in the session would, under most circumstances, be the right course of action to take for number 6 on the above list as well. The experience and feelings you had all those years age are *yours*, not your clients and can only get in the way of you being accurately empathic. You must try to 'clear the decks' so that you can see your client clearly and understand *their* experience, not the echoes of your own.

*If you think that your feelings are due mostly to the client's behaviour then share your feelings with the client. Be honest with a little tenderness. Introduce your feelings by saying that the feelings are yours and explain what it was that the client did that they seem to be linked to. The purpose of doing this is to offer the core condition of genuineness and it may well also be useful feedback to the client about the likely effects of his/her behaviour.

*If you think that your feelings are a mixture of your mood or temperament and the client's behaviour, say so. Be tentative and introduce the issue by saying:

> "I'm not sure why, but I'm beginning to feel bored by what you're saying. I wonder why that is - do you think you're lacking enthusiasm for what you're saying? Does it ring any bells for you?"

The client is then free to think about what you're saying and take it on board or dismiss it as irrelevant. They may even come back to it later.

*Number 10 is a special case for several reasons: **firstly** it is less likely that you will be overcome with passion for a client when you are speaking to them on the telephone, than if you were counselling them face-to-face. **Secondly** it is clear from the various codes of ethics and practice that sexual contact between counsellor and client is forbidden. And **thirdly**, generally speaking if you are using counselling skills, it is not advisable to share feelings of sexual attraction with your client. Some clients may feel attracted to you and should this happen you may prefer to reflect their feelings back to them and seek supervision.

*When appropriate, it is important to let the client know what you're thinking and feeling in a way that adds to their experience rather than subtracts from it. In a way that doesn't blame the client, leave them feeling rejected, judged or threatened. This is a difficult skill to learn and once again practice with feedback is the only way to perfect this aspect of your counselling.

In Training : One way of raising awareness to the early learning which underpins our lack of constructive openness about feelings is to encourage trainees to look at the whole issue of hurting someone's feelings.

Use experiences in the group to highlight this. Split into threes and ask trainees to remember
i) the last time they were bored with what was going on in the group (but didn't say anything)
ii) the last time they were angry with someone in the group (but didn't say anything)
iii) the last time they felt attracted to someone in the group (but didn't say anything)

Then ask them to
i) remember how they dealt with the feelings;
ii) share in their group of three and
    a) discuss how working on the telephone might affect how they deal with these feelings, then
    b) discuss ways of expressing their feelings without threatening or blaming the other person;

> iii) they may even like to try role playing or
> practising dealing with some awkward situations.
> Make some of the role plays 'unsighted'. Some tutors
> could step in to model their own preferred ways of
> handling such situations.

Communicating non-judgemental warmth.

It sometimes strikes me that most people who offer themselves for training in counselling skills must have a basic level of non-judgemental warmth. I have never yet met a truly cold person in a counselling skills training group. I hope I am not deluding myself and that counsellors are all really like the infamous mythical children's entertainer who hates children.

Even so, it is still a good thing to spend some time raising awareness about non-judgemental warmth. In Chapter 3 I pointed out that there were two components to the core condition of *acceptance* or non-judgemental warmth; the absence of judgement and the communication of warmth. It is not unusual to find yourself getting concerned about the non-judgemental bit of this core condition, since you may quickly realise the potential areas of conflict between being non-judgemental and being genuine.

You may be tempted to think that because you are working on the telephone, you cannot be seen and therefore can 'hide' your judgemental attitudes from the client. Therefore you don't need to do any work on yourself because it isn't needed. **Firstly**, clients are *at least* as sensitive to non-verbal cues over the phone as counsellors. **Secondly**, many clients are *super sensitive* to being judged and will react to the slightest hint of potential judgement from you. And **thirdly**, self-development is a GOOD THING. Don't run away from it. It scares me too, but I know that I'll be a useless counsellor if I don't give my best effort in coming to terms with the pain and joy of getting to know myself better.

It may be necessary to spend some time helping ourselves unravel the facts, fantasies and feelings around judgement. In Chapter 3 I mentioned the *johari window* as a way of understanding self-awareness and personal development. The issues surrounding judgement in our lives are best tackled by using the powerful joint action of self-disclosure and feedback from others. In training this is best achieved through exploring our attitudes to sensitive moral issues in personal development sessions and receiving feedback from others about how we come across in general and when counselling clients

> In Training : It is sometimes necessary to raise some sensitive issues deliberately if none come up in the normal course of events during a training programme (eg your own moral dilemmas) to start discussion in the group. Sometimes it feels safer for participants to split up into twos or threes for this. The characteristics to facilitate are openness, flexibility and willingness to challenge and be challenged constructively without blaming.

The sorts of issues that are well-known no-go areas for 'polite' discussion are the ones which we will have to face as counsellors. Try testing your feelings about some of the following:

- Abortion
- Violence in general
- Rape and male violence
- Explicit sexual talk
- Racism - are you racist?
- Swearing, blasphemy and bad language
- Gay love/sex between people of the same sex - are you homophobic?

- Pre/extra marital sex
- Suicide
- Contraception
- Helping the police
- Sexism - are you sexist?

It is practically certain that you will be confronted by a number of these issues in your role as a counsellor even though you may have been successful in avoiding them in your life up to now. As a counsellor you will have to be flexible, understanding and accepting of other people.

If you are rigid and inflexible, not only will your clients not be helped by you, you yourself will also have a hard time since in nature rigid, inflexible things tend to snap and break under pressure.

Most of the cues used in the communication of warmth involve voice quality, so it is particularly important to concentrate on warmth in the voice for people who will be working on the telephone. Once again the best help you can get here is feedback from others on what you sound like when counselling. One of the best ways of doing this is to tape-record some practice sessions with fellow counsellors or trainees and play these back in small groups or just to yourself. What do you sound like? (Yes, I know it can be a shock for many people when they hear their voice on tape. Instead of a deep, reassuring, manly, mid-atlantic drawl, I hear my thin brummie whine!)

•How do you and your colleagues rate your voice on warmth and why?

•What characteristics of your voice would you want to change?

•What qualities of the voices of others do you admire?

In Training : To introduce the concept of non-judgemental warmth, split the group into pairs then ask trainees to think of a person in their lives with whom they associate 'warmth'. This person would be someone who has give them warmth and might even be the epitome of warmth for them -

What qualities does this person have, what is it about them that communicates warmth?

Then think of a person who is the exact opposite of warmth, the antithesis of warmth -

What qualities does this 'anti-warmth' person

have? How do they communicate 'anti-warmth'?

Share in pairs, then after forming a mental picture of each person (warmth and anti-warmth) think of two key words that they associate with each person. Collate key words and share in large group.

Stage 2 and 3 Skills

You may be wondering why the Stage 2 and 3 skills have been unceremoniously lumped together and squashed into a few lines at the end of the chapter. To refresh your memory, here is a re-run of them as they were earlier in the chapter:

Stage 2

Understanding: Helping the client see their situation with new understanding, from different perspectives, with alternative information.

Skills: All of Stage 1 skills plus summarising, linking and integrating issues into themes, offering new perspectives, sharing, challenging, immediacy (looking at what's happening right here and now between you and the client) and goal setting.

Stage 3

Action: Looking with the client at possible ways of acting in this situation. Assessing risks and possible outcomes. Helping the client evaluate the effectiveness of their new behaviour.

Skills: All of the skills of stages 1 & 2 plus brainstorming, creative thinking, planning, implementing and evaluating plans.

The telephone neither adds nor takes away from these skills. The real effects of the phone are limited to those relationship building skills we find in Egan's Stage 1, which are the same as Carl Rogers' three core conditions of empathy, acceptance and genuineness. If you can successfully build a helping relationship over the phone by putting the three core conditions in place, you will have created an excellent stage on which to perform Stage 2 and 3 skills. Neither you nor your client will be hindered by the phone. It will have become 'second nature'.

5 Problem Calls

Back in 1972 when I first sat down in front of the telephone as a 'telephone counsellor' it seemed to me as though every call was a problem call. In many ways this was a very healthy frame of mind and one that it will pay you to maintain when using counselling skills on the telephone. Complacency is at worst dangerous and at best means that your clients are not getting the most you can offer.

After a few calls however, it may become clear that some calls are more problematic than others. This is not to say that you will stop hearing all clients as unique individuals, it's just that some situations will recur and you may well wish to develop some helpful strategies so that you don't have to keep 're-inventing the wheel' every time the telephone rings. This chapter will show you some of the more common situations which cause heart searching and head scratching at telephone counselling agencies all over the country.

I'd like to start with a reminder regarding problem calls on the telephone. Remember Chapter 1 of this book? The Most Useful Question? Whenever you feel suck or stumped by circumstances ask yourself, and those around you if there's anyone there:

What would I do in this situation if it were face-to-face?

On many occasions, the answer will become clear either at this point, or after a bit of thought or discussion. I also believe that the very best answers will come from yourselves, taking into account your own , your agencies and your clients circumstances, personalities, foibles and needs. Don't be afraid of inventing you own wheels! I've taken four types of call which I have seen cause problems in the past, both for myself and others, and offered a few pointers which I hope will help you and your clients.

Silent Calls

There are three types of silent 'events' in telephone counselling.

Silences : pauses in reciprocal conversation of varying length in a call when the caller does not speak,

Silent Calls : a call which begins with silence at the caller's end and continues in silence at the caller's end for a varying length of time until either you (if agency policy permits) or the caller ends the call,

Silent Endings : when after a call of varying length in which the caller has spoken, the caller falls silent and remains so for a varying length of time until either you (if agency policy permits) or the caller ends the call.

All three types of silence can last for seconds, minutes or even in very rare and extreme cases (depending upon your agency policy) for hours.

> In Training : Split into small groups and ask the question What might be happening on the other end of the phone when the caller is silent? What explanations can you come up with?

Face-to-face counsellors may have noticed something strange here. The term 'silence' as used above clearly doesn't mean *silence* in the face-to-face sense. In face-to-face counselling the term 'silence' means a period during the interview in which *neither* the client *nor* the counsellor speaks. I am using the term 'silence' to mean a period during which the client or caller doesn't speak. This means that one of the golden(ish) rules of counselling which all new counsellors pick up and beat themselves with, ie *thou shalt not interrupt a silence*, is thrown out of the window.

The two prime objectives of the counsellor are to establish and maintain contact. These are the first two steps in forging a therapeutic relationship. When you are denied visual contact and are

connected only by a telephone, the only way this can be achieved is
to do so verbally. Put bluntly, you've got to talk to your client even
though they may be remaining silent. This doesn't mean, though,
that you should engage them in *conversation* any more than you
would if you were in a face-to-face situation.

As I have mentioned before, when you lose visual contact with your
client and you have a degraded sense of hearing (until telephonic
engineering improves sound quality) you need to establish some
basic pieces of information for yourself:

Is your client still there?

Why are they not speaking?

How are they feeling?

What are they trying to communicate to you?

Can you hear anything? If yes, what?

What do you make of what you can hear?

At the same time as attending to your own requirements, you will
need to establish some basic pieces of information for your client;
remember they can't see you either! Such as:

You (the counsellor) are still there.

You are listening.

You can hear some sounds.

You care very much about what is happening.

You are ready to respond in a sensitive way.

You want to respect their silence as much as possible whilst maintaining contact.

There is no great mystery surrounding these things. I have found the most simple ways are nearly always the most effective. In Chapter 4 I looked at the core conditions for counselling and one was genuineness. You may like to develop some ways of establishing contact with you client through silences in ways which are genuine for you. Ways which most suit you as an individual.

Personally, I have found an honest and direct approach to be the best. Try saying:

"I'm still here."

"I'm still listening."

"I want to hear what you have to say, if you want to carry on."

"Are you still there?"

"Tap the phone if you are still there."

"I can hear you breathing."

"It sounds as though you're crying."

"I thought I heard someone come into the room, do you want to carry on talking?"

"It's OK to say nothing, I'll just wait until you're ready to carry on."

"I'll keep reminding you that I'm still here and still listening."

You will find that you will have to speak reasonably frequently. Just saying, "I'm still here" once, won't do, it will sound odd and awkward. If you perservere, you will develop a good 'flow'. Try using a watch with a second hand to check how frequently you are talking (it's OK to do this during the call, your client can't see you!) Too much talk from the counsellor is just as damaging to the quality of contact as too little. Depending upon what you can hear at the other end (breathing, sobbing, chattering teeth, softly whispered mumblings, or nothing at all) I have found that saying something every 15 to 45 seconds is about right. My own timing often depends upon how I'm feeling just as much as on what's happening at the other end of the line.

In Training : In pairs, one person closes their eyes and remains silent (the 'caller') the other person, (the 'counsellor') with a watch which counts seconds in front of them, speaks into the silence trying to make and maintain contact. Both members of the pair then give feedback to each other on how it felt. Discuss in the large group.

Issues for the 'counsellor' : what made you want to speak or keep quiet?
How often did you have to talk in order for you to feel comfortable?

We need to return to the three types of telephone silent event.

In a **Silence**, the task is to keep contact with the client. Having already established contact, you must let the client know you are still there listening and at the same time satisfy yourself that the client is still there as well. Your next task is to try and understand the silence. Don't try to interpret the silence; silences mean different things to different people and at best your 'interpretation' is a guess.

You might be able to understand the silence by thinking about what the client said last, listening to any background noises and listening to any sounds your client might be making. You could then feed this back to your client either one at a time or putting them together. In this way you can incorporate the silence into the counselling session, possibly enabling your client to work through the silence constructively.

Silences are perfectly natural elements in human interaction, but in counselling they can be more frequent and sometimes indicate that something particular is happening for the client. The telephone makes working with these silences more difficult but if you try out some of the suggestions above, you may find them less daunting.

Silent Calls. These can be much more demanding than a silence. This may be because so many of us have experienced the 'threatening' version of the silent call at home. Under such circumstances a silent call is a menacing intrusion, an invasion of our privacy and safety. No wonder we get worried when a caller remains silent after we've delivered our opening "My name is ......can I help you?" patter.

> In Training : Ask the group to share experiences of threatening silent calls. Possibly split up into pairs to talk about the feelings involved. Then look back at the reasons generated for why people might be silent on the phone and discuss why we might feel differently about the two situations.

In a silent call, your task firstly is to make contact before you can even consider maintaining it. The first thing to do is to avoid getting hooked into the sort of feelings and behaviour you might have should you get a silent call at home. Don't say impatiently "Who's there...I can hear you breathing...I know someone's there!!" Try saying:

* *"Hello....is there anyone there."*

* *"I can't hear you....I'll wait for you to start talking."*

* *"If you are nervous just take your time...I won't hang up on you."*

* *"Tap your phone to let me know you're there."*

**"I can hear you breathing/crying......I'll wait as long as you want me to."*

As before, you may want to time yourself if the silent call lasts any appreciable time. In fact you will shortly face the most awkward problem in a silent call....*when to end the call.* How long are you prepared to (or allowed to) listen and respond to a person who is remaining silent on the other end of the phone. What has got to happen before you are convinced that they are not there anymore or not interested or even asleep? I have had many callers fall asleep on the phone in the early hours, though it's not terribly difficult to recognise the familiar sounds of snoring!

If you decide that you are going to end the call, your task is to be genuine, whilst not leaving the client feeling rejected.

- Tell the caller that it's OK to be silent if that's what they want, but you have decided to end the call.

- Tell the caller why you are ending the call (there may be other callers waiting, you are tired, you need to go to the toilet, it's agency policy to limit the time of calls, etc).

- Say that you are happy to talk to them again at any time (give your agency availability times).

- Remind them of your number.

- Give them a last chance to say something (they might even say 'Goodbye').

- Say, "I'm putting the phone down now...Goodbye".

Silent Endings : These have largely been covered in the section on silent calls above, but there is one difference between silent calls and silent endings. In a silent ending, you may know who the client is and you will know something of their problem since you will have been talking to them. This does change things slightly. It's almost the equivalent of a client getting up and walking out on a counsellor in the middle of an interview in a face-to-face setting. Whilst this is quite rare in a face-to-face setting, it is not so rare for a telephone counsellor to be 'left' by a client falling silent and remaining silent.

> In Training : How differently do counsellors feel about silent calls and silent endings where the client's identity is known?

The techniques for dealing with silence in this situation are the same as those mentioned above. The difference is how you may feel about it. Try saying:

"Are you still there.....I don't know why you are not talking."

"It's really difficult for me to know whether you are still there and wanting to talk."

"I want to be here for you while you are silent, but it's difficult to know whether you want me still to be here."

"Tap the phone if you are unable to talk but want me to hang on."

"I will stay on the line for another two minutes before I put the phone down."

You may feel reluctant to put the phone down on a client who you feel close to, and you may feel strong feelings of rejection if such a client puts the phone down on you. If that happens, you will have to prepare carefully for the next time you speak to them.

Abusive or Threatening Calls

I have already mentioned the link in some people's minds between silent calls and threatening calls. It is easy to see how this link is made in our everyday experience as phone users. This is also reinforced by films and TV drama which prey on the fantasy notion that the caller can actually see us or has some knowledge of us simply by phoning us. Of course, the caller may know some things about you such as your address and may make a guess about your gender, but other than that they are mostly in the dark.

Sooner or later every telephone agency receives calls in which the (usually anonymous) caller threatens the listener and women seem to receive more abusive calls than men. Because we are offering a caring service where there is often the unspoken ethos 'The client is always right', we are often more vulnerable. We become paralysed, trapped between our need to care for the caller and our fear and revulsion at the threats made against us.

> In Training : Check to find out how many people in the group expected to receive threatening calls. How do people feel about the prospect? Encourage trainees to share their feelings about threat and any experiences they may have had if it feels safe enough to.
>
> At this point, outline your agency policy. If anyone withdraws from training at this point, check with them that they are feeling OK. No-one should be blamed or be left feeling inadequate if they can't handle difficult or abusive calls.

What should we do when threatened on the phone? The first thing to do is to ask yourself The Most Useful Question.

Then ask yourself:

"How do I feel about abusive or threatening calls?"

"Do I want to listen to abusive or threatening calls in general?"

And remember:

You don't have to listen to anything you don't want to.

If the agency you work for has a policy which seems to insist that you listen to all calls no matter what is being said on the other end of the phone; remember, you don't have to work for that agency. It's OK to look after yourself.

In general it's also OK to expect agency policy to provide you with a safe and secure working environment, so find out your feelings on abusive calls and then you will know what to ask for. See Chapter 3 for more on agency policy.

Of course, it's also reasonable for an agency to have the general policy that volunteers and workers should never put the phone down on a caller. If this is the case I would expect them to back this policy up with adequate training and selection so that workers know what to expect, are trained to deal with it and are not made to feel a failure if they don't want to work in this way. Also, agencies with such policies should provide good readily available support (see Chapter 6) for those occasions when counsellors feel overwhelmed by a call. This is much more likely to happen during or after an abusive or threatening call which they are required to listen to.

If your agency does *not* require you to listen to abusive or threatening calls, I would then expect your training to have prepared you to end such calls in a way which does not take away your dignity or safety and which still has the client's needs firmly in sight. It might be too threatening to try and empathise with a violently abusive caller in real life, but for the purposes of preparing yourself for such a call, you may find it helpful to remember that the client must be doing this for a reason that makes sense to them.

In Training : If your agency does not require workers to listen to abusive calls, how do you recommend they end the call? (You may tell them to put the phone down immediately without saying anything.) Do not reveal your agency policy at this stage.

In a safe, secure group (either split into threes or leave as a large group) ask trainees to brainstorm ways of ending an abusive call? People will often have favourite ways of doing this when they have received such calls at home.

Allow enough time for trainees to talk through feelings associated with violence, threat or abuse which may be brought up by this activity.

Now introduce your agency policy and discuss in the light of trainees' thoughts and feelings.

For those who have never received a threatening or abusive call, it's difficult to explain quite how frightening an experience it can be. My own early experience of such calls was to react with fleeting surprise followed quickly by a mixture of fear and anger. I felt like getting stuck in and 'sorting the caller out' in a combative way. How dare he (I have never personally received a threatening call from a woman, though I know it does happen) threaten me when I was giving my time to help on this counselling line!

Thankfully, I was not *required* to listen to threatening calls, and over a period of time, with support from others on duty with me, I was able to put the phone down without wanting to fight the caller.
As soon as the phone was down, I would experience a flood of fear

which would stay with me for hours sometimes, particularly if I was on duty alone and unable to talk it through with someone else. Abusive and threatening calls still trouble me, leaving me with sticky feelings which, although they go after a while, are much better dealt with by having good on-line support (see chapter 6).

In Training : Experienced telephone counsellors will know that abusive and threatening calls, whilst not frequent, can be a common experience. Workers must be prepared for this.

If your policy is to take such calls, you have to prepare workers thoroughly to listen to the calls, engage the caller and most importantly, not get damaged by the process. This requires good training and good support systems. This book does not provide a complete training programme, just training hints and tips. If you don't know how to provide such preparation through training, employ a training consultant who does.

Skills development and personal growth for trainees go absolutely hand in hand in this area of training. Always give enough time for trainees to talk through their feelings about threat, violence and abuse. Only use trainers who can handle this themselves.

In a safe secure group (split into threes or remain in a large group). A good exercise to start off with is to ask trainees to write down as many unpleasant, abusive, threatening and menacing sentences as they can think of. Share in the whole group and write up on a flip chart. Discuss in whole group.

If you do choose to listen to abusive or threatening calls you must answer the question **Why?** before proceeding. Some reasons might be:

• *"I am a caring person and I want to be unconditionally warm to all callers and clients regardless of their behaviour."*

• *"I am used to being abused and insulted. It's like water off a duck's back to me."*

• *"People are basically good and there must be a reason why this person is being abusive. If I can understand the reason, maybe counselling can help."*

• *"It doesn't bother me. I'm not easily offended."*

• *"I quite like being spoken to like this."*

• *"Listening to phone threats will help my personal growth."*

On balance my experience has shown me that people *are* basically good and that if I can provide the core conditions and the client wants to change, then counselling can help. I do not believe that people are abusive without a reason.   If I can talk to them for long enough without getting too angry or frightened myself I might be able to understand what they are trying to say through their threats and abuse. Of course, that's what I *think*. What I *do* in any given situation may easily depend upon how I feel at the moment a call arrives. Whether it's because I've had an argument with my children, or Aston Villa have lost to Birmingham City, I need to be able to 'listen' to myself and if I feel vulnerable, remind myself that **I don't have to listen to this stuff.**

Simply deciding that you don't have to put up with anything you don't want to is no protection from the shock of the unexpected. And if you do decide that you are prepared to listen to such calls, there is the small question of what to do when it happens. So what might you do when you are minding your own business, the phone rings and the caller says "I know where you live and I'm going to fucking slit your fucking throat you bastard!"

If you decide to take the call:

The first thing to do is

> *listen very carefully.*

Don't worry, you won't get 'drawn into' the caller's world of violent threats or 'infected' by their violence. Most people, quite sensibly, 'close down' to abusive calls so that they can't hear the horrible things the caller is saying. Do the exact opposite; turn up an imaginary volume control in your head so that you catch all of the subtle nuances in the caller's speech. This will have two effects:

1. If you are surprised, shocked, frightened or nervous it will help get rid of your immediate nerves, giving you something to concentrate on.

2. It will reveal a richness of detail in the 'standard abuse' which will give you the opportunity to understand more about the caller's world and feed back more to him/her. It will help you hear the caller as a unique individual, something it's very difficult to do when they're being verbally threatening, abusive and violent.

Then:

> *remember your task is to offer the core conditions.*

It's easy to forget this in the heat of the moment, so remind yourself - Empathy, Warmth and Genuineness. At the same time, remember you're not there just to be the passive butt of someone else's bile.

In Training : Try presenting the trainees with some abusive, threatening language. It's sometimes too much to expect people to both say and listen to abusive language in the same exercise, so make a tape of yourself or another trainer saying some threatening or violent things. Split up into threes, tell the groups that they can hold hands if they wish, for some extra support. Play the tape to the whole group, sitting in threes. Talk about responses and feelings in the threes then discuss in large group.

Exactly how you strive to be genuine, empathic and non-judgementally warm under these trying circumstances will depend upon what your agency offers, your personality, how you feel at the time and what the caller is saying.

Common Ground?

Abusive or threatening calls are, for many people, linked with calls from telephone masturbators. (See below.) This link can be a personal, theoretical or political one:

Personal: to receive either type of call is very unpleasant indeed and can leave you feeling invaded, abused, conned, duped, or even raped even. A call from a man wanting you to talk about your body and sexual preferences whilst he masturbates would be extremely threatening to most people.

Theoretical: both kinds of call fall into the same category of event for many people, ie a distorted expression of the need to dominate others through humiliating them. This view may well lead to ideas about how to respond to such callers.

Political: Both types of call are further evidence of male violence since the vast majority of these calls are made by men. After listening to a few from men and even fewer from women, there is, in my experience, a different quality to the calls made by women.

This could, however, be due to my inability to step outside my standard perceptions and responses in terms of heterosexual, gender-based stereotypes.

There is the view that this behaviour is a 'cry for help'. Whether you hold that view or not, such abusive or overtly sexually involving behaviour when expressed over the telephone is certainly a piece of human communication. All communications are made with the expectation of a response and I believe that my responsibility as a counsellor is to give a response that

- is as free as possible from the clutter of my own fears;
- is as clear and unequivocal as I can make it;
- adds to the clients experience rather than takes away from it;
- leaves the client feeling that s/he has encountered a real person with real feelings;
- does not leave the client feeling that their behaviour is either approved of or disapproved of;
- does not reject the client as a worthless person.

The above holds true whether or not I decide to listen to the call. Even if I decide to not listen, I would like to put the phone down in a manner congruent with the above aspirations. In other words, in the very act of not listening and putting the phone down I will be trying to offer the core conditions of empathy, warmth and genuineness. If I decide to listen to the call, I've somehow got to deliver the core conditions for the duration of a call in which the caller is trying to involve me in their sexual fantasies, either directly or indirectly.

Whatever your view, if you do make a link between abusive, threatening calls and those made by telephone masturbators, you may well decide that a similar response is required for all such calls. I think that a common set of principles applies to all calls and that the type of call is largely immaterial. I hope that view comes over clearly as you read through this book. However, I feel strongly about the element of personal choice here. As a counsellor I am not obliged to listen to anything I don't want to. I am not expected to make a personal growth issue out of this either, I won't try to tackle it, like Everest, just because it's there. And I do not have to apologise to anyone for my views or decisions.

> In Training :Provide plenty of opportunity to talk this whole issue through. Many views will be represented in the training group and there must be enough of the right quality time and space to give everyone who wants, a chance to talk. If anyone withdraws from training at this point, do follow them up with a call or letter, offering them a chance to talk and either withdraw or re-join the training without feeling a failure. (This should also happen if anyone withdraws at any time for any reason.)

Telephone Masturbators

When I first volunteered to work on a telephone counselling line, I never imagined that people might phone up and want to listen to someone talking to them whilst they masturbated. Maybe it came as a shock to you too? It didn't take me too long to get used to the idea in theory, since I also believed that only women would be prey to telephone masturbators. I was wrong.

It is true to say that the majority of callers wanting to say or listen to sexually explicit language whilst masturbating require a female to take part, a small minority either want a man or don't care who they talk to. Most callers wanting this are men, though I was completely taken by surprise by a caller purporting to be a woman on one occasion a few years ago.

To those who are familiar with this type of call, there are some distinguishing features:

> *Some callers are excited by the element of surprise or deceit. They appear to want to 'con' the listener, engaging you in

sexually explicit conversation without letting you know that they're masturbating. They never let the language get crude enough to betray their activity and they try to conceal their climax.

*Other callers are crude from a very early point in the call, asking blunt personal questions about clothing, parts of the body and sexual preferences - what colour knickers have you got on, are your tits big and do you like to suck big cocks? These callers may not try to conceal their masturbating or their climax.

*As mentioned above, some callers use directly violent, abusive and threatening language.

Ten years ago the problem of telephone masturbators was high on the list of priorities in training for telephone counselling agencies. Since then we have seen the advent of telephone 'chatlines' and they do provide a service which has taken the pressure off telephone counselling agencies to some extent in some regions. Callers who are 'upfront' about their sexual demands in a telephone conversation may now be more likely to phone a chatline where they can guarantee finding someone who will play along and indulge their fantasies. Although such chatlines are monitored, I believe that in reality, most callers' needs are likely to be met.

The issues surrounding how to deal with telephone masturbators are practically guaranteed to cause feelings to run high. One way or another people will react strongly to the prospect of receiving such a call. Some people are so shocked and outraged that they refuse point blank to talk about it or even think about it. These strong views and feelings reflect the strong reactions felt by counsellors when they receive such calls. Outrage, shock, abuse, violation of self and downright anger are all common reactions, however experienced the counsellor might be. These strong feelings are the starting point to help us decide whether we are going to listen to these calls or put the phone down as soon as we realise what's going on.

In Training : The following information is given
earlier in this chapter when dealing with abusive
and threatening calls:

Experienced telephone counsellors
will know that calls from persons seeking sexual
gratification whilst not frequent, can be a common
experience. Workers must be prepared for this and
the first step is to help them decide if they want to
listen to this type of call.

If your policy is to take such calls, you have
to prepare workers thoroughly to listen to the calls,
engage the caller and most importantly, not get
damaged by the process. This requires good
training and good support systems.
Skills development and personal growth for
trainees go absolutely hand in hand in this
area of training. Always give enough time for
trainees to talk through their feelings about
sexual violence Only use trainers who can
handle this themselves.

In a safe secure group (split into threes or remain in a
large group). A good exercise to start off with is to
ask trainees to write down as many sexually explicit
sentences as they can think of. Share in the whole
group and write up on a flip chart. Discuss in whole
group.

Then in pairs, explore feelings about these calls, each
partner should help the other to approach a decision.
Re-convene large group, share what it was like.

If you do choose to listen to calls from people wanting sexual gratification you must answer the question **Why?** before proceeding. Some reasons might be:

•*"I am a caring person and I want to be unconditionally warm to all callers and clients regardless of their behaviour."*

•*"I am used to this kind of language. It's like water off a duck's back to me."*

•*"People are basically good and there must be a reason why this person is behaving like this. If I can understand the reason, maybe counselling can help."*

•*"It doesn't bother me. I'm not easily offended."*

•*"I quite like being spoken to like this."*

•*"Listening to explicit sexual demands will help my personal growth."*

"Men need to get relief somehow and I'd rather they phoned up like this than go out and rape someone."

Just reading these questions will start you thinking about your motives. If you answer them as honestly as possible it will help you avoid falling into the trap of using counselling work to get your own needs met at the expense of the caller.

> In Training : If your agency policy is to listen to such calls or give your workers the choice, the agency must support this position with adequate preparation, support after calls and supervision.
>
> There is no substitute for practice in real life, it is a little difficult to arrange for this category of call.

Role-plays are about as near as you will get to the real thing and even then you will need to take care:

*Prepare the trainees for the role play by warming up with some sexually explicit talk. Get trainees to brainstorm as many sexually explicit words as they can. Put up on the flipchart. How did that feel?

*Ask trainees to brainstorm as many sexual acts and words for them as possible. Put up on flipchart. How did that feel? Was it easier or more difficult than the last time. (See earlier in this chapter.)

*Ask trainees to volunteer for the role of caller, then split into pairs for a role play back to back. Ground rules could include the idea that the counsellor can stop or hang up anytime and help could be on hand from experienced counsellors if anyone is upset by the exercise. Role play should last 5 minutes maximum.

*Share in pairs then de-role thoroughly. Share in large group. Check that trainees stay out of role during large group discussion.

*Try the above steps 'cold' without the warm up stages. (In real-life the calls come in without warning.)

*Pay careful attention to creating an atmosphere of empathy, warmth and genuineness in the group and allow plenty of time for discussion. In any event this is good modelling of the core conditions in a counselling relationship and should be a constant aim in training.

The suggestions I have made for training are not a recipe for success, but you may find them useful as guidelines if you have not trained workers specifically to receive abusive, threatening or sexually explicit calls before. The process can be put into a nutshell as:

• Awareness raising

                                    Using personal development
• Decision making

                                    as the main vehicle throughout
• Skill development

A group atmosphere of warmth and trust is essential if your trainees are to experience this as a positive learning opportunity, rather than an opportunity for gratuitous sex talk or to make a political point or just to scare volunteers off! Getting the balance right may take some time, but openness on the part of the trainers goes a long way to ensuring a productive, positive training event. Good luck!

Third Party Calls

"Hello? My friend is pregnant and doesn't know what to do. How do you get an abortion?"

"I'm sure that my niece is being abused by my sister's new boyfriend and she's only six. Should I call the police, social services or what? Will you do it for me?"

"There was terrible screaming and shouting from next door half an hour ago, some loud bangs then it all went quiet. Please can you get an ambulance? I'm worried that someone's been hurt. Please call one now."

"I'm only phoning 'cos I'm desperate. He keeps me locked up in the house all day because he thinks that if I go out some man will look at me and I'll be off. It's a stupid idea and he knows it, but ever since he had the operation he thinks I won't love him anymore. He needs help and if he doesn't get it soon I *will* be off! What can you do to help us?"

All of the calls above touch onto the issue of 'third party' calls to a greater or lesser degree. A third party call is one in which the caller is seeking your involvement, or help, on behalf of a (usually anonymous) person who is not present - the third party. The key words here are 'seeking your involvement', since the experience of receiving a third party call is as close to feeling 'hooked' as you can get. Just like a fish you may feel tempted to take a bite but beware, you may get caught and end up in a net!

So great is our desire to help that sometimes we try to help where it's not been asked for. This is the dilemma of a third party call. The person who seems in need isn't there and can't be asked if they are in need of help or, if truly in need, whether they want help, and if help is genuinely wanted, whether they would choose you. All of this discussion about their life is happening without their knowledge or permission, and in their absence.

Whilst we are attending to the business of the third, absent person we are missing the opportunity of working with the real client. The one on the end of the phone. In both face-to-face and telephone counselling situations,

your client is always the person you're talking to.

Some simple guidelines might help deal with these awkward situations:

> *Ask yourself "Just who is the client here?" whenever you suspect you might be getting drawn into counselling a third person.

> *Consult agency policy as to whether third party calls are responded to at all, eg, you should report all cases of suspected abuse or you should call an ambulance if you think someone's life is in danger.

> *Take appropriate action to deal with the request for help if permitted by agency policy.

*Get your counselling head back on and offer the core conditions to the client at hand.

Of course these are fine words but how do you actually do it?

> In Training : Use the examples on the previous page to generate discussion about the general issue of third party calls. Then introduce agency policy. Use the examples again to get trainees to suggest ways of dealing with different types of third party calls.

Try this yourself now. How would you respond to the above calls? Use the guidelines mentioned on the previous page taking note of the possible pitfalls. Here are the calls again:

Hello? My friend is pregnant and doesn't know what to do. How do you get an abortion."
Pitfall: Don't immediately assume that the caller is really talking about herself.

"I'm sure that my niece is being abused by my sister's new boyfriend and she's only six. Should I call the police, social services or what? Will you do it for me."
Pitfall: Don't start a discussion about the relative merits of police vs social services and what you would do if you were the caller.

"There was terrible screaming and shouting from next door half an hour ago, some loud bangs then it all went quiet. Please can you get an ambulance? I'm worried that someone's been hurt. Please call one now."
Pitfall: Don't get freaked out by the thought of someone lying injured somewhere. If the caller was so concerned s/he could always dial 999 for an ambulance themselves.

"I'm only phoning 'cos I'm desperate. He keeps me locked up in the house all day because he thinks that if I go out some man will look at me and I'll be off. It's a stupid idea and he knows it, but ever since he had the operation he thinks I won't love him anymore. He needs help and if he doesn't get it soon I will be off! What can you do to help us?"

Pitfall: Don't get involved with the third person by asking questions to satisfy your natural curiosity like "What was the operation he had?" etc.

Throughout this exercise remember

i) to refer to your agency policy or your own personal policy on third party calls and

ii) who your client is:

Your client is always the person you are talking to.

Hoax Calls

Hands up if you worry about what to do if you receive a hoax call? Have you ever received a hoax call? What is your agency policy about hoax calls? Do you get more hoax calls from young people messing about?

By the way, just what *is* a 'hoax call'?

Some of you reading this will be convinced that you can answer this question and you've probably spent a lot of time which you feel has been wasted listening to children giggling, burping and farting down the phone at you, or just blurting out the odd rude word or two, or remaining silent, or giving a contradictory account of their problem.. To dismiss these and other types of behaviour in children and adults as 'hoaxing' may well cause you to miss the one call in ten or twenty from a person in genuine need. The child being physically or sexually abused, the adolescent on the brink of suicide through bullying, or the woman desperately trying to pluck up the courage to report a rape.

Some agencies and individuals set about the task of trying to distinguish between such valid calls and the real hoaxers. Indeed some agencies will even alert workers to well known 'hoaxers'. Such a quest is, in my view, useless. It is based on the false premise that you can know enough about the caller from a few seconds on the phone to make an informed decision. It is further based on the incorrect view that people in distress act in a stereotypically distressed way.

In the early sixties, the American psychologist Stanley Milgram conducted a now famous experiment in which he led volunteers to believe that they had just killed another volunteer in the experiment by giving him ever larger electric shocks until he died of a heart attack. The interesting part for me was not that the majority of ordinary people could be persuaded to electrocute a fellow human being, but how they reacted to the process of the experiment and the realisation they had killed someone. The experiment was recorded on film. What do you think they did? How would ordinary people react?

Well, they reacted in just about every way you could think of. Some cried, some exclaimed "My god what have I done" or "Oh no, this is terrible". A clergyman sat in dumbfounded silence and one man laughed. He couldn't stop giggling; in the middle of the horrific situation he snorted and sniggered like a schoolboy. He giggled all the way through, shock after shock, as his volunteer partner (in the next room) screamed and begged him to stop. There could be, however, no doubt that given my view of the whole scene, I could see that the man in question was giggling through extreme distress.

There's no way of telling how people will react to stress and our task of understanding what's going on for the caller is made all the more difficult because counsellors can rarely see the whole scene, especially when working on the telephone.

If a caller is behaving in an inconsistent, contradictory or just inexplicable way, don't be too quick to label them as time wasting, manipulative or a hoaxer. Doing this is an attempt by you to make sense of their world from *your* point of view. Your task is to seek the information from *their* world of experience which will make sense of their behaviour.

In the vast majority of cases, people behave in a way which makes sense to them. (This does not mean to say that they are not in distress, hurt or frightened.) Some counsellors hold the view that people *always* behave in a way which makes sense to them at some level. I generally agree with this view. My task as a counsellor is to find the sense in the client's experience and then I will be able to understand them.

This might sound a bit like Mission Impossible, but it's not that difficult, it takes a little patience and some non-judgemental warmth. These two qualities were missing in private eye Jake Gittes, the character played by Jack Nicholson in the film Chinatown. He confronts Evelyn Mulwray played by Faye Dunaway over the identity of a mysterious young woman, central to the plot. Mrs Mulwray's evasive behaviour and apparent deceit takes Jake Gittes to the edge of violent frustration.

"Who is she?" he asks as he shakes Evelyn.
"She's my daughter," she answers.
More lies, thinks Jake and he slaps Evelyn across the face in frustration, hoping to get to the truth.
"She's my sister," Evelyn gasps as Jake slaps her face the other way.
"She's my daughter."
Slap!
"My sister."
Slap!
"My daughter. She's my sister *and* my daughter!"
Evelyn collapses, looks away from Jake and sobs.
"My father and I................Understand? Or is it too tough for you?"

Jake Gittes had found the clue which helped him understand the contradictory information. As counsellors, our methods may not seem as direct, but we must not let our frustration get in the way of holding all contradictions until we understand the client's world well enough for them to be no longer contradictory.

There is no such thing as a hoax call.

6 After the Call

The very first call I ever took (at the age of 20 after twelve weeks 'training') was from a caller who mistook the counselling service where I worked as a volunteer, for Dial-a-Prayer. After some initial confusion on both our parts it turned out that the caller had a terminal illness causing great pain, had had both legs amputated and to cap it all her husband had recently died. She had taken what she hoped was an overdose of barbiturate sleeping pills and wanted a kind voice to read prayers to her as she slipped away.

We talked for a while after which she asked if I would read The Bible to her (I am not a Christian). After a frantic search of the office and a stroke of luck, we were able to find a copy and I read her favourite passages to her until my asking her what I should read next (I am not a Christian) got no reply. She would not tell me her number nor where she lived. She told me only her name and that she thought that it was time for her to be with her husband.

After listening intently for and signs of life at the other end of the phone I turned to the other counsellor on duty with me (he was a catholic priest and had gathered that something unusual was happening from my anguished expressions and the Bible hunt). He pointed to the chair on which I was sitting and as I looked down I saw the trousers I was wearing were literally soaked in sweat. It looked as if I had wet myself. I wasn't quite sure what I was feeling. I didn't know what to do next. I gave a quick nervous laugh and then cried in his arms for what seemed like hours. The training course had not prepared me for this.

I had learned how important it is that counsellors have access to support whenever they want it, whatever their working situation.

In Training : Try presenting this scenario as a case study and asking trainees to debate the professional/agency policy issues involved. What would *they* do in this situation? What do they think it is *correct* to do? Try asking the following questions:

*Does my agency policy support me in my decision to listen and talk to an apparently dying woman?

*Should I have called the police, ambulance or asked for assistance?

*Should I have tried to persuade her to tell me her address so that I could rescue her?

*Should I have had my fellow counsellor in the same room as me when the call was in progress?

This chapter is about what counsellors may need to do after a call in order that they and their service can survive until the phone rings again. To return to my car journey analogy for a moment, it's the equivalent of what you need to do after you've parked the car and turned off the ignition. For example, make sure you take your valuables out of the car and lock the doors. If you noticed any faults develop during your journey or a refill is required, these will have to be attended to before you take the car out again. What sort of end-of-session servicing do you require before you can go back on the road again?

Whether you work for an agency or on your own, you will need to have these things in place in some form or other; don't kid yourself that you can cut corners. If your agency doesn't attend to these issues, agitate for change, provide them for yourself or don't work there. The three areas which may require attention after the call are boundaries, on-line support and record keeping.

Boundaries

The above account raises a number of issues. In terms of boundaries, many of the issues such as confidentiality/privacy hark back to those chapters covering how we might arrange things before and during the call. However, I have found that the same issues arise again the second I put the receiver down. Also, although I have separated 'boundaries' from 'on-line support' and 'record keeping', there is overlap between all three as I will try to demonstrate.

When I put the telephone down on a counselling session, I often experience a deep desire to talk about the call. This desire is frequently complemented by an equally strong desire on the part of other counsellors on duty to be told about the call. However we might try to dress these urges up as some kind of professional development or 'spot supervision', the truth to be faced is that we like to have a good natter about the work that we do. We would do well to ask ourselves some questions about these desires:

• Why do I have the need to talk about clients?

• What aspects of an individual call is it most helpful to talk about?

• What feelings do I have about this caller and his/her life?

• How should I talk about another person's personal life?

• Where is it best to talk about the content of individual calls and my reaction to them?

In Training : These are obvious questions to ask trainees when introducing the need for on-line support, regular supervision or confidentiality and office routines

As I have pointed out in Chapter 3, privacy is different from confidentiality. In this situation we are talking about confidentiality; the need to keep the client's business within the boundary set by the interview. Set against this is the occasional need for a counsellor to get support if the client's problem is particularly distressing for the counsellor concerned for whatever reason. This distress can take many forms and almost always happens when the client's problem triggers an emotional reaction in us such as anger, hurt, disgust or guilt because the problem reminds us of some sensitive issue in our own life such as unresolved grief. Sometimes of course, a client's problem can be just too overwhelming (that's why they've phoned a counsellor for help) and we have difficulty in listening to it without feeling over-whelmed ourselves. This sets up a tension between our need to keep a promise of confidentiality and our need for support.

If the agency I work for offers a confidential service (see Chapter 3) then I believe that I must honour that in between interviews. I do not want to talk about my clients in a disrespectful way in the guise of seeking support. I resolve this tension by following certain rules when getting on-line support (see below).

Particular calls can put us under pressure to think that the boundary of the interview should be broken for other reasons. For example if we are lead to believe that the client/caller is in danger or that a third party is in danger. 'Danger' can mean almost anything here from physical or sexual abuse through to self harm or suicide. The question is "What should I do?" If I manage to get through the majority of the interview without intervening, the panic really sets in when the call seems to be coming to the end :

> "Can I really let this person go and do whatever I fear they might do?"

And it gets even worse as soon as the receiver goes down :

> "Did I do/say the right thing? - What if...(insert terrible outcome here).......happens; it will be all my fault.

I should have persuaded them to give me their address
and called the police/ambulance/Samaritans.
Dash it, we ARE the Samaritans!"

I often think it would be great if I could shout "TIME OUT!" in the
middle of a call and get some spot supervision.

> In Training : This is a good exercise in any training
> session. Encourage trainees to call time out in practice
> sessions in front of the group and let them get
> spot supervision from the tutor.

Unfortunately, it is not possible to do that, although there is much to
be said for letting the client know that you are upset/uneasy or lost in
the middle of a call (see Genuineness in Chapter 4). What I can do
though is get on-line support from a colleague, backed up by supervision later.

On-line Support

Anyone who has worked for any counselling agency, will know how
important this kind of support is. Whether it comes from your peers
or a day officer/supervisor it doesn't matter. As long as you get it *when
you need it.*

There are no rules to **giving** this kind of support; just offer your
counselling skills to the person sitting next to you; and don't be afraid
of physical contact when your colleagues are feeling very needy. A hug
goes a long way when support is wanted. Remember that such support
times have their own boundaries of confidentiality too.

When **seeking** support, I find the following rules of thumb help me to
avoid the gossiping trap I referred to above:

•I want to talk about, and preferably express, my feelings rather than
talk about the client or their feelings.

•If I must talk about the client, I want to do so respectfully. I want to talk about them and their world as I would wish my own most tender secrets talked about.

•Who or what in my life does the client and their world remind me of?

•What do I need to do, or talk about, right now so that I can decide whether to take another call or withdraw from duty for the rest of the session?

•What issues do I want to take to supervision as a result of this call?

If I can stick to these rules I stand a reasonable chance of meeting my immediate and urgent need for support and making the most of a potentially wonderful learning situation. Of course it goes without saying that in the heat of the moment when I most need my helpful rules, I am least likely to remember them. If these rules seem to make sense to you, or you have some good ones of your own, share them with your colleagues and incorporate them in to your training. In this way the colleagues to whom you go for support can act as your memory for you. You might even consider sticking the rules up on the office wall.

Record Keeping

I suppose there are many candidates for the "Good-idea-in-theory-but-not-done-in-practice" award when it comes to agency policy and one of the strongest contenders would be record keeping. We all say we will do it, we all tell our colleagues we do it, we all kid ourselves that we really *do* do it. But we don't, at least not as frequently and as completely as we should.

There are a number of good reasons why keeping records is a good idea:

1. As a memory aid. When you get any sort of decent case load, you'll find that your memory soon becomes exhausted. You can refresh yourself before a client is due in a face-to-face interview or quickly get a client's file out when they phone up for a counselling session. Always have the record file within reach of the phone or or the phone on a long lead!

2. Personal and professional development. Good records can be a boon in supervision and will prove indispensable if you apply for BAC accreditation as a counsellor. Also, when you get long in the tooth and want to publish your grand theory of counselling, you will want to refer back through your case records to pull together the evidence. I really wish I'd kept mine!

3. Lies, damned lies and statistics. If you ever need to justify your existence as a counsellor you will suddenly appreciate the need for evidence of effectiveness and efficiency. The basis for much of what managers feel is acceptable evidence are accurate records. In the 1990's this holds true as much for voluntary organisations fighting for funding as it does for local government services.

4. Monitoring. Similar to number 3, monitoring is for example checking your clients (and staff) to see that you are fulfilling your promises to be an equal opportunities service or that you really are meeting the needs of your target client group.

5. It is agency policy. Ah yes, well, there's no getting away from this one. If you agreed to keep records you can't really carp about it now.

6. Protection. If a client complains that they have been damaged in some way by your service, it will help to have accurate records of your relationship with dates and times etc.

These good reasons for keeping records raise some ethical, personal, and possibly legal, issues.

As far as the **legal issues** are concerned, these are relatively straight-forward. Firstly, before you put any information on a computer which may include the names and addresses or telephone numbers of clients or staff, check if you need to register under the Data Protection Act. Secondly, see Chapter 3 in which I briefly outline the legal position on confidentiality and security of information. Other people including the police have few legal rights to any information you hold even when a serious criminal offence may be involved. Finally on the legal side, you have to consider your client's rights to seek damages from you if you have promised to keep their records confidential and fail to do so. For example, if your office was burgled and your files were to get into the wrong hands, details of your client's lives and identities could leak out causing distress.

Ethical and personal issues are more complicated since we each bring our own personal values and ethics to the situation along with those we adhere to as responsible counsellors. I have chosen the following to illustrate some general issues. You may well have special concerns of your own.

Some counsellors feel that record keeping is not in accord with their personal qualities and say something like, "I am a caring counsellor and will remember every single detail of all of my client's lives forever." Others may feel that record keeping in some way contaminates their theoretical position and skill base and say something like "Keeping records will encourage me to think in general terms and categorise my clients. When I next speak to them, I might only remember the false categorisations, not the real person."

I offer the following suggestions regarding record keeping which may help overcome these and other reservations you may have. The key to secure records is to never keep all of the information relating to one client in the same physical place. When I say 'physical place' I mean different filing cabinets, different rooms or different parts of a computer programme which can never be combined on the screen or which require different passwords to gain access.

I prefer to split the information up into three pieces each recorded on cards in a card file as follows:

Card 1:   Name   Client number
             Address
             Telephone number home
             Telephone number 2
             Telephone number 3
             Telephone number 4

Keep these cards in alphabetical order - they are your **Contact Cards** and would be used if you want to contact a client for any reason whatsoever or more usually if you want to locate their other files. You may be wondering why there are four telephone number options. Some agencies will phone a client back to save the client the expense and hassle of putting coins into a call box. (Nothing is worse that trying to talk about your problems when you are more concerned about your money running out.) If your client is a regular caller, s/he may have favourite locations from which they call, you can make a note of these on the card rather than writing the numbers down each time they call.

Card 2:   Name   Client Number
             Brief Address:
             Demographic details: eg Age, sex, ethnic origin, disabled employment status etc for monitoring purposes.
             Referred from: eg Self, other agency etc
             Referred to:
             Presenting problem:
             Coded list of problem types eg
                  1=financial
                  2=accommodation incl homelessness
                  3=personal/sexual
                  4=personal/educational etc
             First session date:
             Counsellor: (some agencies have numbers or codes)
             Final session date: (leave blank if still having sessions)
             Counsellor:
             Return date: (if client re-presents, start another card)
             Counsellor:

These are your **Statistics and Monitoring Cards** and should be kept in client number order. The list on the card is not meant to be exhaustive, but it gives you an idea of the kind of information it may be useful or necessary to collect. You will be able to discover how many women and men used your service, what the age profile of your clientele is, whether your service is used by different ethnic groups, who refers the most clients to you, which areas of town they come from etc. This information will be invaluable in

i) your annual report to justify your funding, and

ii) your analysis of the effectiveness of your service.

It's always more interesting to see who doesn't use your service, rather than who does. This will tell you whether you are really open access (if that is your aim). You may need to find out why four times as many women aged fifteen to twenty phone up than any other age group.

Card 3	Call record	Client number
	Dates: Times:	Duration:
	Issues discussed:	
	Action taken:	
	Counsellor:	

These cards are the **Case Note Cards** and should also be kept in client number order. Note that the clients can't be identified from this card alone, and although they can be identified from the other cards, no-one can tell why they have contacted your service, since the presenting problem section should be in your code. These cards are useful for case discussions and reviews, group supervision, agency planning, and statistical reporting since you will be able to show how many client sessions the agency provided, how many each client had on average etc.

There's one final type of record that I like to keep and that's my own personal log or counselling journal. I keep my personal record of each client contact session both on the phone and face-to-face. Clients can be referred to by any code you choose. I allocate one sheet to each session and divide the page up into three sections:

1. What the client talked about.

2. How I felt today - how I felt towards the client, was the session very tiring, was I bored, excited, distracted etc.

3. How I thought I performed in the session today; what supervision issues were raised by the session.

I know that a number of counsellors keep similar personal journals and I can highly recommend it as a good method of getting the very best out of your supervision sessions and turning every session with a client into a potentially wonderful learning experience. It also helps avoid the problem of letting my thinking become too rigid and compartmentalised through all this record keeping. The process becomes much more personal, fluid and creative and makes a great contribution to my personal and professional development.

7 Between Calls

This chapter is concerned with the between-journey maintenance all cars need to stay on the road. What do we as counsellors need to do between duties or clients to maintain ourselves, to prevent burnout and to continue to develop ourselves so that we continually improve? These activities are differentiated from those mentioned in the last chapter by virtue of the fact that these are not related to the last call you received. These activities are to do with your process of being a counsellor.

I could put such activities into categories like on-going professional development (eg training), ongoing personal maintenance and development (eg personal therapy) or burnout avoidance etc , but I prefer to not compromise the importance of any of these activities by dividing them into categories and then having to choose between them. Instead, I suggest that counsellors might make a single space which has the potential to achieve all of this and a good deal more besides. Such a space is called **supervision**.

This suggestion is not new. Supervision and support have been written about in many places throughout this book and, as I have also pointed out, supervision is now universally recognised as an essential component of a counsellor's professional activities. By 'professional' I do not mean that you have to be paid for your counselling, rather that if you consider yourself to be a counsellor or using counselling skills substantially, then your work should be of a professional standard.

What is supervision?
Many people engaged in counselling (or helping in general) have found their own ways of getting support. Maybe through talking to friends, colleagues, family etc. Such informal arrangements have a few drawbacks, firstly they are OK for emergencies but lack any real

potential for learning and development and secondly confidentiality is always a problem. The third disadvantage is that however devoted to you and your work they are, your family and friends may soon get sick of it.

The word supervision is another word which whilst becoming more common in helping settings, it is still prone to misinterpretation. Some suggest it would help if we said 'counsellor supervision' instead, but I think that this may limit a brilliant idea to the select few. Supervision used in this context does not mean line management, does not imply control, permission or discipline, is not linked with authority or direction and has little to do with the idea of overseeing probation or trial periods.

Counsellor supervision has the following elements:

•Facilitation of personal and professional development.
•Personal and professional support and challenge.
•Promotion and development of counselling skills.
•Maintenance and development of ethical practice.
•Promotion of accountable counselling practice and services.
•Congruence with counselling values.

In my case, as a Person-Centred counsellor I have chosen a supervisor who shares my theoretical orientation. I expect my supervisor to provide the core conditions in supervision. These are the conditions which I believe are necessary before any beneficial support, learning or development can take place. I expect to meet my supervisor as an equal but with different roles in the relationship.

Many people worry about the boundaries of supervision, what is acceptable and valid as a supervision issue and what is not. As far as I am concerned, anything which arises from or is affecting my work with clients is fair game. Everything from discovering that the reason I am getting nowhere with my client is because she reminds me of my ex-wife to being depressed because I'm fed up at work and even including whether Aston Villa won on Saturday.

Who, where, how and for how long?

This book is not about supervision, but I do know that very few agencies or individuals providing a telephone service pay enough attention to supervision. They fall short of good practice because they believe they haven't got the resources to provide adequate supervision. Whilst I (as a supervisor and supervisee) know that supervision, like counselling is a skill that takes time to acquire, I also know that many voluntary organisations must do the best they can with what they've got. It is in recognition if this that I offer the following suggestions.

General guidelines
> •Supervision should not be less frequent than once per month otherwise the lack of continuity will be too disruptive to the development of a good supervisory relationship.

> • 0 -5 clients/sessions per week requires around 1 hour supervision per month,
> • 5 - 10 clients/sessions per week requires around 1 hour supervision per fortnight,
> • 10 - 20 clients/sessions per week requires around 1 hour supervision per week.

> •Several supervisees together with one supervisor at the same time is called group supervision. It doesn't save a huge amount of time since each supervisee should be allocated nearly the same time pro-rata as in individual supervision. There are other benefits though.

> •Get hold of a copy of the BAC Code of Ethics and Practice for Supervisors.

Co-supervision
Co-supervision is seen as a popular solution when the money is short. What happens is this: two counsellors agree to pair up in a co-supervision relationship. Each supervision meeting lasts say two hours, each taking one hour as supervisee, whilst acting as super-

visor to the other for the remaining hour.

Support Group

I've not called this a 'supervision group' because I really do think that it's too skilled a task for inexperienced counsellors. Working in a group has several benefits. Development of social skills, learning through exposure to a wide range of views and experiences, seeing many different ways of solving problems and that sense of *belonging* are all available only through working in groups. A support group could orient itself towards supervision issues by having regular meetings which were carefully boundaried. No gossiping, socialising or tea-making. Participants could take responsibility for bringing 'supervision' issues and being supported by the group whilst they explored the issue they had brought.

Support Network

An extension of the supervision group whereby after exchanging telephone numbers and addresses we agree to give 'spot support' if something arises out of our work with clients between support group meetings.

Special Training Events

One of the things that happened to me after I finished my counsellor training was that I felt a great thirst for more training. It was a combination of i) feeling lost without the chums I had spent a year going through thick and thin with, and ii) thinking that I had only just chipped the surface of counselling skills and that there was so much to learn!

Occasional touchdowns to training are a good idea since no training is a complete preparation. Intermittent special events for counsellors in an agency help counsellors express their commitment to on-going professional development and help the agency update their workers on new developments, specialist areas or whatever. A programme of meetings advertised well in advance is the best way of doing it, sometimes inviting guest trainers if funds allow.

The Ideal Solution
Put simply, the best plan for delivering supervision and support on a budget is to arrange co-supervision and a support group running in parallel. The support group could then join up with others in your agency for the occasional special training event. If your agency does not have a system of support and supervision, there's nothing to stop you from organising one yourself. The minimum you need is a willing partner and you're off. Add four more and you've got a support group.

Hints for first-time supervisors
If you are setting up a co-supervision relationship or support group for the first time and you've never been a supervisor or experienced supervision as a supervisee before, here are some simple guidelines to help you:

• Don't be afraid, if your intention is to create a safe environ ment in which you can help your partner learn from their experience, you won't go far wrong.

• Set off with the further intention of offering the core condi tions to your partner.

• Listen carefully to what they are saying; seek clarification if you're not understanding fully.

• Help them explore their concerns using role-plays, looking at notes, talking to imaginary clients or whatever method seems appropriate.

• Can you see any links or connections between the issues and concerns that s/he brings.

• Look for patterns of feelings, thoughts and behaviours in what your partner is saying and in their work with their clients.

• Ask your partner if what s/he is saying sounds familiar to them or has echoes in other areas of their lives.

• Challenge your partner to look deeply into their experience. Don't be afraid to question what they are saying.

These guidelines work just as well in a support group, where you may decide that the role of 'facilitator' is to rotate from meeting to meeting or be shared by all group members.

Whatever you decide to do, good luck and remember that your basic tool-kit is you and your core conditions. You are never without it. Do not sell yourself short on support and supervision, your life may depend upon it. We are all now familiar with the term 'burn-out' and it has been suggested that one of the main causes of burn-out is insufficient opportunities for supervision, support and continuing training. Ways of avoiding it include making arrangements for support and supervision, attending training workshops, looking after your physical health and bringing variety into your counselling work. All of these remedies can be monitored through supervision.

References

British Association for Counselling, *Code of Ethics and Practice for Counsellors.* BAC Rugby.

Inskipp, Francesca, (1986) *Counselling: The Trainer's Handbook.* Cambridge: National Extension College.

Rogers, Carl R. (1961) *On Becoming A Person.* London: Constable.

Appendix

Useful Addresses
British Association for Counselling, 1 Regent Place, Rugby, Warks., CV21 2PJ.

The Advice, Guidance and Counselling Lead Body Secretariat, c/o Julie Janes Associates, 10a High Street, Welwyn, Herts., AL6 0RN.

Youth Access, Magazine Business Centre, 11 Newarke Street, Leicester, LE1 5SS.

Further Reading
Egan, G (1981) *The Skilled Helper : a model for systematic helping and interpersonal relating.* Monterey Ca : Brooks Cole.

Egan, G (1982) *Exercises in Helping Skills.* Monterey Ca : Brooks Cole.

Mearns, D. and Thorne, B. (1988) *Person Centred Counselling in Action.* Sage.

Munro, E.A. et al (1983) *Counselling: A Skills Approach.* Aukland, New Zealand : Methuen. (Revised Edition).

Murgatroyd, S. (1985) *Counselling and Helping.* London : BPS and Methuen.

Rogers, Carl R. (1961) *On Becoming a Person.* London : Constable.

Rogers, Carl R. (1980) *A Way of Being.* Boston : Houghton Mifflin.